1200

D0101964

ℰℰ
Classic Collection
Carolina

The author George Sand and her lover Frederick Chopin were among the first tourists to visit Mallorca in search of sunshine and peace. During the winter of 1838/39 they stayed in Palma and in Valldemossa and their experiences are described by George Sand in her own subtle way. They both admired the beauties of the island, which we are able to share with them.

GEORGE SAND (1804-1876) was one of the first women of her generation to live an independent life with energy and verve. She was a contemporary and friend to many famous people of the time. She made a name for herself as a critical novelist and was an example to others.

George Sand

A Winter in Mallorca

Revised translation
of the original
by Shirley Kerby James

Classic Collection
Carolina

Revised English translation
of the first French edition
Un hiver à Majorque (Paris 1842)

This book is available in the same design
in German "Ein Winter auf Mallorca"
ISBN 84-89983-50-X
in Spanish "Un invierno en Mallorca"
ISBN 84-89983-51-8
in French "Un hiver à Majorque"
ISBN 84-89983-53-4

© 1998 by Classic Collection Carolina, Meudt/Germany
1^{rst} edition: Novembre 1998
2nd edition: May 1999
3rd edition: March 2000
Design: P&C, Pollença/Mallorca
Preprint: Serveis de Preimpressió, Palma de Mallorca
Printing and bookbinding: HenarGraf, Madrid

ISBN 84-89983-52-6
DL: B-33582-98
Printed in Spain

PREFACE

George Sand and Frederick Chopin both appreciated the sun that draws so many people to Mallorca. nowadays. They also wanted peace and quiet in order to devote their time to their creative work undisturbed.

As George Sand wrote, she felt the need to escape her daily routine, like so many people do today, and to recuperate and concentrate on all the things that there is never enough time to do. All this sounds very familiar to us, for we don't say without reason that somebody is "ready for the island".

The relationship between George Sand and Frederick Chopin began in the summer of 1838 and helped him to forget his unhappy love affair with her predecessor. In the autumn of that year, after a bad cold, the artist was left with a serious cough. The doctors recommended him a warm, sunny climate which they also prescribed for George Sand's son,

Maurice, to ward off further attacks of rheumatism.

This seemed a good enough reason to spend a holiday together, and originally they planned to go to Italy. Later they changed their minds and on the recommendation of their Spanish friends, Mendizábal, Marliani and Valldemossa, they decided on Mallorca. This gave them a chance to be be together all the time, as Chopin normally lived in Paris, while George Sand had to return regularly to Nohant to see her husband and her family. George Sand, incidently, is the pseudonym of Aurore Dupin, baroness Dudevant. Chopin was surprisingly enthusiasted about the trip, considering he normally hated any changes in his daily routine. He liked every day to be exactly the same, so that nothing interfered with his sensitive mental harmony. He also disliked the idea of being separated from his piano, his friends, his doctor and particularly his social life. It required a loving and much loved person to drag him away from Paris.

They travelled separately to Perpignan. George Sand and the children left in the middle of October and made the journey in easy stages, stopping to visit friends on the way. Chopin followed later with his friend Don Juan Mendizábal, taking the fast coach and making the journey in four days (!), which he survived remarkably well. They travelled by ship from Port Vendres to Barcelona because it was too dangerous to continue the journey on land due to the civil war in Spain. After a short stay in Barcelona, they made the crossing to Mallorca in 18 hours, under conditions that would be difficult to imagine nowadays. In her book, George Sand describes the unbearable conditions with her usual humour and irony. The voyage was recorded in the logbook of the steamer "*El Mallorquin*" on 7th November 1838, which listed all the passengers travelling first class as well as those travelling second class, and included the maid Amelia. The account given by George Sand gives us no reason to believe that there were different classes of passenger on board. These records survive today in the Royal Historical Archives in Palma. The date of their return journey with the same steamer is recorded as 13th February 1839.

George Sand carried an unlimited letter of credit issued to the Bank Canut in Palma. The banker's wife, Hélène Choussat, later described their visit and the effect it had on the people of Mallorca. For a start, this foreign lady signed herself with a man's name! What's more, both George Sand and her daughter ran around in men's shirts and trousers. Otherwise she almost always wore black or very dark colours. It was quite unusual enough to find an unmarried couple living together with the children, both artists and therefore accustomed to deference and respect. Thus, it becomes clear that a deep rift separated the aggressive Madame George Sand from the conservative and deeply religious Mallorquins and her vicious and ironic attacks on them can be attributed to the same cause. The banker's wife does acknowledge however that the islanders were still deeply rooted in their traditional ideas and that they had only just begun to venture beyond the island and to see some more of the world, since the purchase of the steamer.

At the same time, a certain shyness towards the artists must have played a significant part, for Madame Choussat did not even dare to ask George Sand to write a dedication in her autograph book. Although she did help them in another matter: When the time came for their departure Chopin and George Sand were faced with the problem of what to do with the Pleyel piano, that had so much trouble to bring with them? The banker's lady bought it and sold the one she always owned. At least she didn't believe in Chopin's tuberculosis, like the fearful Mallorquins, or perhaps she didn't care.

After the fiasco with the house of Señor Gomez in Establiments, both Chopin and George Sand were delighted with the cell in the charterhouse at Valldemossa, where they finally found refuge. In one of his letters, Chopin wrote enthusiastically that he was about to move into an admirable charterhouse in the most beautiful place of the world. There he would live and dream and compose in an old monk's cell. Later on, he was to describe the cell as an outsized coffin in a dusty barrel vault, with one small window through which he could see orange trees, palm trees and cypresses. His bed was opposite the window below the rosettes. There is still some controversy among scholars over which particular cell he occupied.

To date, both cell 2 and 4 claim to be the one that housed Chopin and George Sand. One of them contains the Pleyel piano which is in fact the actual piano that Chopin played. In the other is the Mallorquin piano that he used according to George Sand's account, before the other one arrived. The prior's cell was not numbered until the cells were sold off separately. So it was even more difficult to find out. A contemporary of theirs has written that he visited them in cell 4 or 5. Anyway both these cells contain interesting and valuable objects from the Carthusian monastery as well as from George Sand and Chopin's visit.

George Sand described Chopin in her biography (which was published after his death) as a very sensitive and sensible man. He composed some wonderful preludes at the charterhouse that expressed his feelings. He appears to have become rather despondent as a result of his illness and to have taken every problem far too seriously. At the same time, the monastery was a place where all sounds and thoughts as well as the weather begged to be expressed in music. According to her biography, George Sand often found "her sick one" overexcited and beside himself when they returned from some excursion. Then he would play to her and the children the music he had composed duting these fits of emotion. In the end, his health deteriorated to such an extent that their visit had to be cut short.

You will find the most beautiful descriptions of nature in George Sand's writing, as well as her ideas. Even when she promises to record only the facts and mention her own experiences only as an example, time and again her agile pen escapes from these limitations. References to her French and Spanish friends are deliberately kept in context or restricted to footnotes which is part of her style and the taste of the period. Nevertheless, in the translation I have tried to make it easier to understand. Besides 'Mallorca' and 'Mallorquin' have been written in the orginal version of the country.

Now, let her take your on an adventure to the Mallorca of the last century, which only a person as strong minded and determined as George Sand could have attempted. Much of what she writes is still valid, despite the advances in mass tourism. The beauty of the island has survived many onslaughts but not all of them. There are still sleepy corners where time has stood still. As far as the Islanders are concerned, her description is not quite correct. A tourist is always welcome because they depend on tourism for their livelihood. Even today, when some Marjorcans fear that there are too many foreigners on the island, particularly Germans, and that they will buy up the whole place, Mallorquins will always treat anyone well who behaves like a corteous guest. Anyone, who speaks a little Spanish can have a wonderful holiday or, as a resident, get to know the large, extended families that exist among the Islanders. He will be welcomed but always within the limits of the natural reservation of Islanders.

Monsieur,

Il y a plus d'un mois, que j'ai reçu une lettre de Pleyel relativement au piano, — j'ai retardé ma réponse espérant toujours recevoir de vos nouvelles et je viens seulement de lui répondre que vous avez fait l'acquisition de cet instrument moyennant douze cent francs. — Ma santé étant tout à fait rétablie, je quitterai Marseille incessamment et n'allant pas directement à Paris je crois de mon devoir de Vous prier, pour empêcher tout retard, de vouloir bien

*pour le payement vous adresser
à Paris à Mr. C. Pleyel et Cie.
Rue de Rochechouard No. 20. qui
sont avertis. —*

*Agréez, Monsieur, je vous prie
l'assurance de mes sentiments
distingués*

F. Chopin

Marseille, le 28 Mars 1839

Monsieur Canut

Palma

NOTICE

This book dates from a letter dedicated to my friend François Rollinat and its existence originates from the thoughts expressed at the beginning of Chapter IV, which I can only repeat: 'Why travel, unless you have to?' Today, returning from the same latitudes but crossed at another point of Southern Europe, I give the same answer as I did when I returned from Mallorca: *It is not so much a question of travelling but of getting away; which one of us does not have some problem to avoid or some responsibility to shake off?*

George Sand

Nohant,
25th August 1855

Letter From a Recent Traveller
To a Homebound Friend

Since you must stay at home, my dear François, you believe that I, carried off by my proud and headstrong rockinghorse of independence, have known no greater pleasure in the world than that of crossing seas and mountains, lakes and valleys. Alas! My most beautiful, my sweetest journeys have been made at my own fireside, my feet in the warm ashes and my elbows pressed on the worn arms of my grandmother's chair. I don't doubt that your travels have been equally pleasant and a thousand times more poetic than mine, which is why I advise you not to regret too much the time wasted, nor the discomfort, of sweating in the Tropical heat, nor of icy feet in the frozen polar wastes, nor terrible storms at sea, nor attacks by bandits, nor any of the dangers or hardships you encounter every night in your imagination, without having to take off your slippers and without any greater discomfort than a few cigar burns on the folds of your dressing gown.

To make up for your lack of open spaces and real physical movement, I am sending you this account of my latest journey outside France, certain that you will pity rather than envy me, and find that I have paid dearly for a few bursts of admiration and a few hours of delight wrestled from my bad fortune.

This account, written a year ago, has earned me a most violent and comic tirade of abuse from the inhabitants of Mallorca. I am sorry that it is too long to be published as a sequel to my story, for the tone in which it is written and the charm with which they attack me, merely confirm my views on the hospitality, good taste and tact that the Mallorquin shows towards foreigners. It would justify including it as a curiosity: but who would read it through to the end? And besides, if it is vain and foolish to publish the compliments you receive, would it not be even worse, these days, to make a noise about the insults?

I will therefore spare you that, and confine myself to telling you, as a final comment on the naive inhabitants of Mallorca, that after reading my account, forty of the most competent lawyers in Palma met to concoct between them a terrible indictment against the "immoral authoress" who had dared to laugh at their love of gain and their concern for the education of the pig. I would say that all forty had as much spirit as four.

But let us leave them in peace, these good people so heated against me; they have had time to calm down and I to forget their way of behaving, talking and writing. I only recall five or six among the islanders of that beautiful country whose kind welcome and friendly manner remain in my memory as a compensation and a blessing of sorts. If I have not mentioned them by name, it is because I do not consider myself important enough to honour them with my recommendation, but I am sure (and I believe that I have said this in the course of my narrative) that they also retain an affectionate memory of me and will not believe themselves included in my disrespectful mockeries, nor doubt my sincere feelings about them.

I have said nothing about Barcelona, where we spent several busy days before embarking for Mallorca. To go by sea from Port-Vendres to Barcelona, in fine weather and on a good steamboat, is a delightful excursion. Along the Catalan coast we began to recover the spring air that we had breathed in Nîmes but which had left us at Perpignan; the heat of summer awaited us in Mallorca. In Barcelona a fresh sea breeze cooled the shining sun and swept all the clouds from the vast horizon, framed by distant peaks, which were both black and bare, and white with snow. We made one excursion into the countryside and the good little Andalusian horses which took us needed a good feed of oats to get us back under the city walls in time to avoid any unwanted encounters.

You know that at that time (1838) the whole country was overrun with wandering bands, who barred the roads, invaded towns and villages, ransacked even the humblest homesteads and occupied villas not half a league from the town, appearing unexpectedly from behind every rock to demand of a traveller his money or his life.

We ventured however to several places along the coast, and met only detachments of Christians on their way to Barcelona. We were told that they were the finest troops in Spain, quite handsome men and not too badly turned out, considering they were returning from a campaign; but both men and horses were so thin, either with such guant, yellow faces or with their heads so low and their flanks so hollow, that one felt pangs of hunger just to look at them.

Sadder still was the sight of the fortifications built around even the smallest hamlet and before the poorest cottage door; a little wall of dry stones, a large battered tower as thick as nougat in front of each door and the small parapets surrounding every roof, which showed that no inhabitant of this rich land felt secure. In many places these small decaying defences showed signs of recent attack.

Once through the formidable and immense fortifications of Barcelona, with I don't know how many gates, draw bridges, back doors and ramparts, nothing would suggest that we were in a city at war. Behind the triple enclosure of cannons and isolated from the rest of Spain by bands of brigands and a civil war, the glittering youth walked in the sun up the "rambla", a long avenue planted with trees and with houses like our boulevards: the women, beautiful, graceful and charming, preoccupied only with the fold of their mantillas and the play of their fans; the men, occupied with their cigars, laughing, talking, eying the ladies, discussing the Italian opera, did not appear to question what was happening on the other side of their walls. But when night fell and the opera was over, the guitars taken away and the city handed over to the careful walk of the nightwatchmen, all that could be heard above the monotonous murmur of the sea, were the ominous calls of the sentries and more ominous still, gunfire at irregular intervals, sometimes one shot, sometimes many, from different places, either repeatedly or alone, sometimes far away, sometimes close by, until the first glimmer of morning. Then everything returned to silence for an hour or two and the citizens appeared to sleep soundly, while the harbour awoke and the seamen began to stir.

If you had dared to ask anyone, during the pleasant hours of their promenade, what the strange, frightening noises had been in the night, they would have answered with a smile that they were of no-one's concern and that it would be wiser not to ask.

FIRST PART

CHAPTER ONE

t was two English tourists, I believe, who discovered the valley of Chamounix, about fifty years ago, according to the inscription carved on a rock at the entrance to the Mer-de-Glace.

The claim is a bit extreme, if one considers the geographical position of the valley, but valid to a certain point if these tourists, whose names I have forgotten, were indeed the first to draw the attention of poets and painters to those romantic landscapes where Byron created his wonderful drama, "Manfred".

In general, it could be said that Switzerland was not discovered by fashionable society or by artists until the last century. Jean-Jacques Rousseau is the real Christopher Columbus of alpine poetry and as M. de Chateaubriand so well observed, he is also the father of romantisism in our language.

Without quite the same claims to immortality as Jean-Jacques and in search for something that I could achieve, I thought that I might perhaps become as famous as the two Englishmen in the valley of Chamounix and claim the honour of having discovered Mallorca. But the world has become so exacting that it would not be enough today to have cut my name into some Balearic rock. I would be expected to produce a fairly accurate description or at least a poetic account of my journey that would tempt tourists to undertake it at my word. But as I felt far from enchanted with that country, I renounced my claim to fame and recorded my discovery neither in granite nor on paper.

If I had written under the strain of all the grievances and difficulties I suffered at that time, I would have found it impossible to boast of my discovery, for anyone reading my account would have felt that there was no point in mentioning it at all. Nevertheless, I have to admit today that there is good reason to mention Mallorca, which is for an artist one of the most beautiful places on earth and one of the least known. When there is nothing but scenic beauty to describe, words are inadequate and insufficient and I would not dare to attempt it. It requires an artist's pencil and an engraver's tool to reveal the splendours of nature to lovers of travel.

If I am now shaking up my fading memories, it is

because of a handsome book I found the other morning on my table, entitled

"Souvenirs d'un Voyage d'art à l'île de Majorque"
by J.B. Laurens.

It has been a real joy for me to rediscover Mallorca in its pages, the palm trees, aloes, Arab monuments and Grecian costumes. I recognised all the places in their poetic colours and recalled my own impressions which I thought I had forgotten. There was not a cottage, nor a bramble bush that did not bring back a world of memories, as they say nowadays, and I felt I wanted, if not to describe my own journey, at least to comment on M. Laurens'. He is an intelligent and hard working artist, who works quickly and conscientously, and who certainly deserves the honour which I had given myself of having discovered the island of Mallorca.

M. Laurens' journey to the heart of the Mediterranean, to those shores where the sea can be as inhospitable as the inhabitants, is far more admirable than the excursion our two Englishmen made to Montanvert. However, if European civilisation ever reaches the stage of doing away with customs officers and police, those visible signs of national dislike and distrust, and if a steamboat could be organised direct from home to these regions, Mallorca would soon become a serious threat to Switzerland. One

27

could get there in the same number of days and certainly find scenery as softly beautiful and as strange and grandiose as in the Alps, which would add another element to the painter's art.

At the moment, I would only recommend the journey to artists of robust physical strength and passionate determination. The time will come, no doubt, when frail amateurs and even pretty women will be able to go to Palma with no more discomfort or distress than to Geneva.

For a long time associated with M. Taylor and his illustrations of the ancient monuments of France, M. Laurens decided, on his own account, to visit the Baleares last year. With so little information about the island, he admits that it was with a beating heart that he landed on the shore, fearing that his dreams might be met with disappointment. But he found what he was looking for and all his hopes were realised, for, I repeat, Mallorca is an Eldorado for the painter. Everything there is picturesque, from the peasant's hut which has retained the Arabic style in its simplest features, to the child wrapped in rags, glorying in its "delightful dirtiness", as Henri Heine described the herbsellers of Verona.

The landscape, richer in vegetation than North Africa but not as spacious, has a naturalness and tranquility. It is as green as Switzerland under a Calabrian sky, with the solemn silence of the Orient.

In Switzerland, streams flow everywhere and clouds move restlessly, over the landscape, creating a sense of movement to the scene which painters are not always successful in reproducing. Nature seems to be playing with the artist. In Mallorca, she seems to wait and welcome him. There, the vegetation takes on strange and odd forms, but has none of the lavish confusion which often blurs the Swiss landscape. The rocky peaks are etched motionless against the glittering sky, the palm tree leans out from the cliff without the breeze disturbing its stately foliage and even the stunted cactus beside the road, everything seems to pose with a kind of vanity to please your eye.

First of all, I will give you a concise description of the largest Balearic island, in the rough form of a note in a geographical dictionary. That is not as easy as one would think, particularly when one looks for information in the country itself. The caution of the Spaniard and the distrust of the Islanders is taken to such an extreme that the foreigner cannot ask the most insignificant question in the world without the risk of being taken as a political agent. The good M. Laurens who dared to sketch a ruined castle that pleased him, was imprisoned by the suspicious governor who accused him of making a plan of the fortress. [1]

After that our traveller, determined to fill his sketchbook somewhere other than the state prisons of Mallorca, was careful not to ask about anything but mountain paths and to research anything other than stone ruins. After spending four months in Mallorca, I would have got no further than he did, if I had not consulted the information that had been written about the region. But here my doubts began again, for these works, already out of date, differed so much between them and, in the manner of travellers, contradicted each other so arrogantly that I have had to resolve certain inaccuracies at the risk of committing many more.

(1)"The only thing that caught my attention on this coast was a dark ochre coloured ruin surrounded by a cactus hedge. This was the castle of Soller. I had hardly finished the outlines of my drawing when I saw four individuals coming towards me with terrifying, though rather ludicrous expressions. I was guilty of making a plan of the castle, which was against the law of the kingdom. At once the castle became my prison.

My command of Spanish was too limited to explain to these people the absurdity of their action. I had to appeal to the French consul in Soller, but despite his insistence, I remained captive for at least three life-long hours, guarded by Señor "Six-fingers" governor of the fort, a real dragon of the Hesperides. I was tempted several times to throw this absurd dragon and his uniform from the top of the tower into the sea, but his expression always disarmed me. If I had Charlet's talent, I would have spent my time making studies of my goaler, a perfect model for caricature. Besides, I forgave him his blind devotion to the safety of the State. It was natural that this poor man whose only other distraction was to smoke his cigar and stare at the sea, should take advantage of the situation I offered to vary his occupation. I returned to Soller, highly amused that I had been taken for an enemy of the country and the constitution (Souvenirs d'un Voyage à l'île de Majorque by J. B. Laurens).

Here then is my entry in the geographic dictionary, and without giving up my role of traveller, I will begin by declaring its unquestionable superiority to all those that have preceded it.

CHAPTER TWO

Mallorca, which M. Laurens calls Balearis Major, like the Romans did, and which the king of Mallorquin historians, the Doctor Juan Dameto, says was once called Clumba or Columba, is now known as Mallorca, a corruption, and the capital has never been called Mallorca, as several of our geographers claim, but Palma.

The island is the largest and most fertile of the Balearic Archipelago, which is the remains of a continent that the Mediterranean must have flooded and which, without doubt, once joined Spain to North Africa, for they share a climate and similar produce. It lies 25 leagues south east of Barcelona, 45 leagues from the nearest point on the African coast and, I believe, 95 to 100 leagues from the Toulon road. The

(1)(Each mile of a thousand geometric paces and each pace of 5 geometric feet. Miguel de Vargas "Descripciones de las islas Pitiusas y Baleares." 1787), total area is 1,234 square miles,[1] the circumference is 143, its greatest length 54, the narrowest 28. The population which numbered 136,000 in 1787, has risen to 160,000 today. The city of Palma has 36,000 inhabitants compared with 32,000 at that time.

The temperature varies considerably according to exposure. Summer is burning hot throughout the plain; but the mountain chain which stretches from north east to south west, (the direction compares exactly with the land masses of Africa and Spain, with corresponding points and angles) greatly influences the winter temperature. Thus Miguel de Vargas reports that in a Palma street during the terrible winter of 1784, the Reaumur thermometer once registered 6 degrees below freezing during the day in January, that on other days it rose to 16 but that it usually stayed at 11 degrees. This temperature was more or less what we experienced during a normal winter in the mountains of Valldemossa, which is reputed to be one of the coldest parts of the island. On the severest nights, after we have had two falls of snow, the temperature was only 6 or 7 degrees. By eight o'clock in the morning it has risen to 9 or 10 and by midday to 12 or 14. Normally, by three o'clock, that is after the sun had set behind the mountains, the temperature would drop suddenly to 9 or even 8 degrees.

North winds often rage furiously and the winter

rain can fall in some years so endlessly and for so long that we in France can have no idea of it.

On the whole, the climate is healthy and kind in the southern part which faces Africa and is protected from the furious storms by a central row of hills and by the steep cliffs to the north. The general plan of the island is therefore a plain that inclines from north west to south east. Navigation is almost impossible in the north due to the steep, jagged coastline, which Miguel de Vargas described as "rugged and horrifying, without shelter or refuge" but is easy and safe in the south.

Despite its hurricans and ruggedness, the ancients had good reason to call Mallorca "the golden isle". It is extremely fertile and its produce is of a high quality. The wheat is so fine and pure that the inhabitants export it to Barcelona where it is made into a light, white pastry known as "pan de Mallorca". The Mallorquins import a coarser, cheaper wheat from Galicia and Vizcaya, so that in a land rich in excellent wheat, the bread is disgusting. I cannot see that this transaction is to their advantage.

In our central area, which is the most backward, the farming methods show nothing more clearly than the stubbornness and ignorance of the peasants. The same applies to Mallorca where agriculture, although meticulously carried out, is still in its infancy.

Nowhere have I seen the soil worked so patiently and ineffectively. Even the most simple machines are unknown. Everything depends on manpower and the men whose arms seem thin and frail compared to ours work with unbelievable slowness. They take half a day to till a piece of earth that at home would take two hours and five or six of the strongest men are needed to move a load that the weakest of our porters could lift gayly on his shoulders.

Despite this laziness, every inch is cultivated and apparently well cultivated in Mallorca. The islanders, they say, have never known poverty, yet with all their natural riches and under their clear skies, their lives seem harder and duller than of our peasants.

Travellers usually write about the good fortune of southern races, whose faces and picturesque clothes seem to remind us of a Sunday in the sunshine. They interpret the lack of ideas and foresight as a simple rustic view of life. It is a mistake I have often made myself. I have abandoned the idea since my visit to Mallorca.

There is nothing as sad or as pathetic in the world as this peasant who knows nothing but praying, singing and working, and who never thinks. His prayer is a mindless formula which seems to make no sense to him; his work is physical toil which his brain seems unable to improve, his song expresses a melancholy of which he seems unaware and whose poetry strikes us without him realising it. If vanity did not wake him from his stupor from time to time and set him dancing, his feast days would be devoted to sleep.

I have already gone beyond the limits I set myself. Strictly speaking, a geographical account should deal, above all, with economic and commercial products and mention only as a last resort, after the cereals and the cattle, the species: Man.

Out of all the geographical descriptions I consulted, I have found this short piece under the heading "Baleares", which I corroborate here, although certain details may have to be reconsidered later: "These islanders are most amiable" (we know that, in every island, the human race forms two categories: those who are savages and those who are "most amiable".) "They are gentle, hospitable; they rarely commit a crime and theft is almost unknown among them." I will certainly return to this text later on.

But after all, we are talking of produce; for I believe that certain words have been spoken recently in the Chamber of Deputies (indiscreet to say the least) on the possible occupation of Mallorca by the French, and I assume that if this book should fall into the hands of any of our deputies, they would be far more interested in the section on produce than in my philosophical thoughts on the Mallorquin intellect.

I have explained that the soil in Mallorca is wonderfully fertile and that a more energetic and knowledgable cultivation would multiply the crops tenfold. The main exports are almonds, oranges and pigs. Oh the lovely Hesperidean trees guarded by these unearthly dragons! It is not my fault that I am forced to add these beastly pigs, of whom the Mallorquin is so proud, to memories of scented flowers and golden apples! But the Mallorquin pig breeder is no more poetic than the deputy who reads my book.

I return then to the pigs. These animals, dear reader, are the finest in the world and Dr. Miguel de Vargas, with naive admiration, gives us a portrait of a young pig, at the innocent age of one and a half, weighing twenty-four 'arobes', which is to say six hundred pounds. At that time, the exploitation of pigs did not enjoy the importance that it has achieved today. Trade in livestock was hampered by the greed of the financiers to whom the Spanish government entrusted, that is to say sold, the victualling business. In virtue of their discretionary powers, these speculators opposed all cattle export while reserving for themselves the right to unlimited import.

This usurious practice discouraged farmers from developing their herds. With meat selling at a low price and export forbidden, they could face ruin or give up cattle breeding altogether. The herds declined rapidly. The historian whom I quote laments the days of the Arab occupation when one hill in Arta could account for more pregnant cows and noble bulls that could be assembled today, he says, on the whole Mallorquin plain.

This was not the only way in which the country's natural riches were plundered. The same writer reports that the mountains, particularly those of Torella and Galatzo, were once covered with the most beautiful trees in the world. One olive tree had a girth of forty-two feet and a diameter of fourteen. But these magnificent forests were devastated by naval carpenters who, at the time of the Spanish expedition against Algiers, built an entire fleet of gunboats from them. The harassment to which the owners were afterwards subjected and the miserly damages they were paid, induced the Mallorquins to destroy their forests instead of increasing them. Today, the vegetation is still so plentiful and lovely that it does not occur to the visitor to regret the past. Now as before, in Mallorca as in the whole of Spain, corruption is still in power. However, the traveller never hears a complaint because, from the start of an unjust regime, the weak man remains silent out of fear, believing that the harm is done, and then continues out of habit.

Although the tyranny of the contractors is over,

Mallorquin livestock has not recovered from its destruction and will not recover as long as the right to export it is limited to the pig industry.

One sees very few cows and oxen on the plains, none in the mountains. The beef is poor and tough. The sheep are of good stock but undernourished and uncared for; the goats, of an African breed, do not yield a tenth of the milk that ours do.

The soil lacks nourishment and despite the Mallorquin pride in their methods of cultivation, I consider that the seaweed they use is a poor fertiliser and that the land is a long way from producing as much as it could, under such a generous sky. I have looked carefully at the wheat which is so precious that the inhabitants do not feel they deserve to eat it. It is exactly the same as we grow in our central provinces and which our peasants call white or Spanish wheat. Ours is just as good despite the differences in climate. The Mallorquin wheat should be noticeably superior to ours, which has to depend on our harsh winters and variable springs. Our farming methods are also primitive and in that respect we have a lot to learn, but French farmers work with an energy and perseverance that the Mallorquins would scorn as chaotic.

Figs, olives, almonds and oranges grow in abundance in Mallorca; but due to the lack of roads in the centre of the island, the trade is far from being as developed or organised as it deserves. Five hundred oranges sell on the spot for about three francs; but to carry this large load on the back of a mule from the centre of the island to the coast would cost nearly as much again. For this reason the cultivation of oranges in the interior is neglected. It is only in the valley of Soller and close to other coves where our small boats can load, that orange trees grow in abundance. They would no doubt be successful everywhere: on our mountain in Valldemossa, one of the coldest regions of the island we had wonderful lemons and oranges, although they ripened later than those in Soller. At La Granja, in another mountainous area, we picked lemons as big as a man's head. I would think that the island of Mallorca alone could supply the whole of France with these exquisite fruit, at the same price as we pay for the horrible oranges we get from Hyère and the Genoese coast. So this trade, which the Mallorquins boast about so much, like the rest is hindered by their superb negligence.

One could say the same about the large olive production, certainly the finest in the world and which the Mallorquins, thanks to Arab tradition, know perfectly well how to cultivate. Unfortunately they can only extract a rancid and nauseous oil which would appall us and which will never be exported in any quantity except to Spain.

In Spain a taste for this offensive oil is equally

prevalent, but Spain itself is rich in olive trees and if Mallorca provided her with oil, it would have to be at a very low price.

We consume a vaste quantity of olive oil in France and we buy bad oil at a high price. If our refining methods were known in Mallorca and if Mallorca had the roads and if commercial shipping was organised to that end, we could have far better oil for what we pay and plenty of pure oil whatever the winter weather. I am quite sure that the industrialists who grow the olive of peace in France would much prefer to sell a few tons of this precious liquid for its weight in gold, so that our grocers can drown it in vats of peanut and colza oil and then offer it to us at 'cut price'; but it would be strange if they preferred to force this commodity from our rugged climate, when twenty-four hours away, we could find better oil at a good price.

However, our French monopolists need not worry too much. We could promise the Mallorquins and I believe, the Spanish in general that we would buy our supplies from them and increase their wealth tenfold, and they still would not change any of their methods. They scorn so forcefully any improvement coming from abroad, above all from France, that I doubt if money (which they do not, on the whole, despise) would induce them to change anything inherited from their fathers.

This oil is so offensive that every house, man and carriage on the island and even the air in the countryside is saturated with its stench. Since it is included in every dish, the smell rises from all the houses two or three times a day and the walls are soaked in it. In the middle of the countryside, if you lose your way, you have only to sniff and if the smell of oil comes on the breeze, you can be sure that behind a rock or under a clump of cactus, you will find a house. If in the wildest, most deserted place the scent pursues you, lift your head and you will see at a hundred paces, a Mallorquin on his donkey descending the hill and coming towards you. This is not a joke or an exaggeration, it is the exact truth.

CHAPTER THREE

Unable to fatten their beef, or use wool, or milk the cows (the Mallorquin hates milk and butter as much as he hates work); unable to grow enough wheat to dare to eat any of it; not bothering to grow mulberries and collect silk; having lost the art of carpentry which used to flourish and is now forgotten; having no horses (because Spain has a maternal claim to all the foals on Mallorca and the passive Mallorquin is not so foolish as to feed the royal cavalry); not considering it necessary to have one good road, one negotiable path on the whole island (because the export rights are left to the whim of a government that has no time to bother with such things); so the Mallorquin vegetated, having nothing better to do than say his rosary and mend his breeches, even more worn than Don Quixote's (his model in poverty and pride), until the pig arrived and solved everything. The export of this animal was permitted and a new era, an era of salvation, began.

In the future, the Mallorquins will call this century the age of the pig, just as the Moslems talk of the age of the elephant in their history.

Now olives and carobs no longer lie strewn on the ground, the cactus fig is no longer a toy for children and mothers of families learn to economise on potatoes and beans. The pig allows nothing to go to waste, for he wastes nothing and he is a perfect example of generosity, combined with simple tastes and habits, that anyone could offer a nation. Thus he enjoys in Mallorca rights and privileges that no-one would dream of offering to humans. Houses have been enlarged and ventilated; fruit left rotting on the ground has been collected, sorted and stored, and steamships, which were considered superfluous and unreasonable, now run between the island and the continent.

It is therefore thanks to the pig that I could visit Mallorca. If I had thought of going there three years ago, the long, dangerous voyage by coaster would have made me give up the idea. Ever since the exportation of pigs, civilisation has begun to penetrate Mallorca.

A pretty little steamer was bought in England. It doesn't have the size to fight against the terrible north wind in these parts but in calm water, it can carry 200 pigs once a week to Barcelona and a few passengers as well.

It is delightful to see how gently and respectfully these gentlemen (and I am not talking about the passengers) are treated on board and how lovingly they are put ashore. The captain of the steamer is a most amiable man who, force to live and talk with these noble beasts, has adopted their tone of voice exactly and even some of their mannerisms. If a passenger complains of the noise they make, the captain will say that it is the sound of gold coins rolling on the counter. If a woman is prudish enough to mention the stench spreading throughout the ship, her husband is quick to point out that money doesn't smell at all bad and that without the pigs, she would have no silk dresses, no French hats and no mantillas from Barcelona. If anyone feels seasick, he can expect no attention from the crew because pigs also get seasick and become listless and lose the will to live and this must be avoided at all costs. Thus losing all compassion and humanity in order to save the lives of their beloved clients, the captain himself, armed with a whip, hurries into their midst with the sailors and boys behind him, all snatching up anything they can find, whether it is an iron bar or a piece of rope, and in an instant the whole herd, lying inert on their sides, is given a fatherly beating and forced to rise and move about against the unhappy rolling of the ship.

When we returned to Barcelona in March, it was stiflingly hot, yet it was impossible to set foot on deck. Even if we had braved the dangers of losing our legs to a bad tempered pig, the captain, I am sure, would never have allowed us to annoy them with our presence. They were very quiet for the first few hours but in the middle of the night, the pilot remarked that they were sleeping too soundly and seemed to have fallen into a black depression So the whip was employed, regularly every quarter of an hour and we were woken by screams and terrible shouts partly from the pain and rage of the beaten pigs and partly from the captain encouraging his men with oaths so that at times we thought that the pigs must be devouring the crew.

When the ship anchored, we tried to get away from this strange company and I swear that the islanders had begun to bore me as much as the others; but we were not allowed to get any fresh air until the pigs had been unloaded. We could have died of suffocation in our cabins without anyone worrying in the least, as long as there was one pig left to unload.

I am not afraid of the sea, but a member of our family was dangerously ill. The crossing, the bad smell and the lack of sleep did nothing to lessen his suffering. The captain had no time for us, except to ask us not to allow the invalid to sleep in the best bed in the cabin, because, according to Spanish superstition, every disease is infectious and as the man had already decided to burn the bed in which the invalid slept, he wanted it to be the worst one. We sent him back to his pigs. Fifteen days later, when we returned to France on the *'Phénicien'*, a magnificent French steamboat, we compared the welcome of the French to the Spaniard's hospitality. The captain of the *'Mallorquin'* had grudged giving a bed to a dying man; the Marseillaise captain, not content that the invalid was comfortable enough, lent him his own mattress. When I tried to pay for the passage, the Frenchman pointed out that I had paid too much: the Mallorquin made me pay double.

From this I conclude that man cannot be equally good in every corner of the globe, nor equally bad. Poor character among men is nothing but the result of material poverty. Suffering breeds fear, mistrust, deceit and every sort of conflict. The Spaniard is ignorant and superstitious; consequently he believes in infection, he fears sickness and death, he lacks faith and charity. He is wretched and weighed down by taxes, so he becomes greedy, selfish, dishonest with foreigners. Throughout history we see that whenever he could be great, he has shown greatness but he is human and in his private life, where a man has to give in, he gives in.

I had to explain this before discussing man as I found him in Mallorca; just as I hope I have said enough about olives, cows and pigs. Even the length of this chapter is not in good taste. I apologise to anyone who might be personally offended by it and I will now begin my account on earnest. I thought I had nothing to do but to follow M. Laurens step by step through his artistic journey and now I realise that many thoughts will come to me as I retrace the rough paths of Mallorca in my memory.

CHAPTER FOUR

But since you know nothing about painting", I will be asked, "what the devil are you doing in that miserable gallery?" I would prefer to detain the reader as little as possible with myself and my family; all the same I will often have to use the words "I" and "we" when discussing what I saw in Mallorca: "me" and "we" being the subjects without which the object "Mallorca" could not have been revealed to the reader. I therefore ask him to think of me as totally passive, like a telescope through which he can watch what happens in that distant land, which can best be described by the proverb "I would rather believe you than go there and see for myself." I assure him that I have no intention of interesting him in the problems that concerned me. I have little philosophical interest in describing them here; and when I have formulated my thoughts in that respect, I hope he will realise that I do not expect him to be preoccupied with me in the least.

I will explain to my reader right away why I entered that gallery, and here is my reason in two words: It was because I wanted to travel. And now, it is my turn to ask the reader: When you travel, dear reader, why do you travel? I hear you reply just as I would reply in your place: I travel for the sake of travelling. I know that a journey is a pleasure in itself; but in the end, what forces you to make this expensive, tiring, sometimes dangerous journey, always filled with endless disappointments? The need to travel. Well then, explain to me what sort of need this is, because we are all, more or less, obsessed, and why do we all give in to it, even when we have realised, time and time again, that this same need rides behind us in the saddle and never lets us go, and is never satisfied?

If you don't want to answer, I will be honest and answer in your place. It is because we are never really happy anywhere, these days, and of all the faces of our ideal (and if the word annoys you, the idea is better), travelling is one of most pleasing and the most deceptive. Everything is going badly in public life: whoever denies it feels it just as deeply and bitterly as those who agree. At the same time, divine hope keeps on going, chasing her dream in our poor hearts and always blowing over us this longing for something better, this searching for the ideal.

Social order does not even live up to the hopes of

its defenders, it pleases none of us, and each one goes his way as he pleases. Some throw themselves into art, others into science, most of us amuse ourselves however we can. All of us, when we have a bit of time and money, go travelling or, above all, escape, because it is not so much a question of travelling as of getting away, you understand? Which one of us does not have some problem to avoid or some responsibility to shake off? No-one.

Whoever of us is not absorbed in work or dulled by laziness is quite unable, I believe, to stay long in the same place without suffering and longing for a change. If anyone is happy (and you have to be very special or very stupid to be that, nowadays) he imagines that he could add something to his happiness by travelling; lovers and newly weds leave for Switzerland and Italy just like the birds and the hypochondriacs. In a word, whether living or dying, everyone is possessed with the fever of the Wandering Jew and goes off in search of some distant nest to make love or some shelter to die.

God forbid that I should speak out against this migration of humanity and take my stand in future among those who stay bound to their country, to the land, to the home, like polyps to a sponge! But if intelligence and moral judgment are to progress along with industry, it seems to me that the railways were not destined to take whole populations from one point of the globe to another just because of a fit of bad temper or an attack of nerves.

I would like to see the human race happier and therefore calmer and more open minded, having two lives: one sedentary, devoted to domestic happiness, to the obligations of city life, to study, to philosophical thought; the other active, for honest exchange instead of the shameful transactions we call business, for inspiration in art, for scientific research, and above all for the germination of ideas. It seems to me, in a word, that the usual reason for travelling is a desire for contact, to communicate and exchange ideas with other people, and that there should be no pleasure in it if there is no obligation. On the other hand, it seems to me that theses days most of us travel in search of mystery and solitude and an escape from the shadow in which the society of our fellow men seems to obscure our ideas, whether sweet or painful.

In my case, I set off to satisfy a need for rest, which I particularly felt at that time. Because there is not time for everything in the world we have made, I imagined, yet again, that if I looked carefully, I would find some quiet, isolated retreat where I would have no notes to write, no newspapers to read, or visitors to receive; where I would never have to take off my dressing gown, where every day would last twelve hours and where I could free myself from the duties of polite society, break away from the state of mind under which we all labour in France and devote a year or two to study some history and learn the basics of my language with my children.

Which of us has not selfishly dreamed of leaving, one fine morning, all his affairs, his habits, his acquaintances and even his friends, to go to some enchanted island and live without cares, without troubles, without obligations, and above all without newspapers?

One can seriously say that the Press, that first and last of things as Aesop called it, has created a whole new way of life for mankind, filled with progress, advantages and worries. The voice of humanity that arrives every morning when we wake to tell us how humanity has spent the previous day, proclaiming so many great truths, so many terrible lies, but always recording every step man takes, marking every hour of our lives, isn't it something truly great, despite all the mistakes and misery found there?

But at the same time that it is necessary for the collection of our thoughts and actions, isn't it terrible and even repulsive to hear all the details, when there is fighting everywhere, and the weeks and even months flow with insults and threats, without ever clarifying a single question and without suggesting a sensible improvement? And during this period of waiting, which appears even longer when all the stages are minutely reported, doesn't it often make us wish, we artists who have no say in politics, that we could fall asleep in the bowels of the ship and wake up after several years to welcome at last a new land towards which we find we have been carried?

Yes, indeed, if that could happen, if we could retire from the world and cut ourselves off from all contact with politics for a while, we would be struck when we returned by the progress that had been made in our absence.

But this is not granted us, and when we flee from the scene of action to seek oblivion and rest among people who live at a slower pace and with fewer burning ambitions than we do, we find problems there which we didn't expect and we regret having left the present for the past, the living for the dead.

Here quite simply is the theme of my book and why I bothered to write it, when it was hardly a pleasant task, and as I promised myself, at the beginning, to keep my personal impressions to myself as much as possible, it now seems to me that this omission would be an act of cowardice and I withdraw it.

CHAPTER FIVE

We arrived in Palma in November 1838, in a heat comparable to that of our month of June. We had left Paris fifteen days earlier in extremely cold weather and it was a great pleasure for us, after feeling the first onslaught of winter to leave the enemy behind us. To this was added the pleasure of exploring a town of great character, which possesses several first class buildings of beauty and originality.

However, the problem to finding accomodation soon began to worry us and we realised that the Spaniards who had recommended Mallorca to us as a most hospitable island and rich in resources, were as deluded as we were. In a country so close to civilised Europe, we could not even find a single hostel. The absence of lodgings for visitors should have warned us at once what Mallorca was like compared to the rest of the world, and encouraged us to return immediately to Barcelona, where at least there was one miserable inn, called somewhat pompously, "The Hotel of the Four Nations".

In Palma, one has to be recommended and introduced to twenty illustrious persons, and kept waiting for several months, if one wishes to avoid sleeping in the open fields. Everything possible was done for us, just to secure two small furnished rooms, or barely furnished, in a disreputable sort of place, where foreigners were lucky to find a single camp bed with a mattress, as soft and padded as a slate, a straw backed chair, and as much red pepper and garlic in the food as you wished.

In less than an hour, we had realised that if we were not enchanted with this welcome, we would be considered conceited snobs and troublemakers, or at least pitied as being fools. Bad luck to anyone who is not happy with everything in Spain! The slightest grimace you make on finding bugs in the bed or scorpions in the soup will invite the greatest scorn and rouse universal indignation against you. So we were very careful not to complain and little by little we began to realise what had caused this lack of supply and apparent lack of hospitality.

Besides the Mallorquin's lack of energy and enthusiasm, the Civil War which had ravished Spain for so long, had interrupted all traffic between the island and the mainland. Mallorca had become a refuge for as many Spaniards as it could hold, and the natives, confined to their homes, dared not leave them to go in search of adventure and action in the mother country.

To these reasons must be added the complete absence of industry and the customs duty levied on every object necessary to one's wellbeing. To give an example: For the piano that we brought from France, we were charged 700 francs in import duties: this was almost the value of the instrument. We wanted to send it back, this was not allowed; to take it out of the town (we were living in the country), in order to avoid the harbour dues, which were distinct from the customs dues, that was against the law; to leave it in the town, in order to avoid the export dues, which were different from the import dues, that could not be done; to throw it into the sea, that in the end was all we were allowed to do.

After fifteen days of negotiations, we discovered that instead of taking it out of the town through one gate, it could be taken out by another and we were relieved of another 400 francs.

Palma is equipped to hold a certain number of inhabitants: so that as the population rises, they close up a little more, and seldom build anything else. Nothing is replaced in their houses. Except perhaps in two or three families, none of the furniture has been changed for two hundred years. They know nothing about the dictates of fashion, or the need for luxury or for comfort in life. There is apathy on one hand and obstacles on the other, so they remain the same. They have what is necessary but nothing more. So all hospitality is restricted to words.

There is a popular expression in Mallorca, as in all of Spain, to avoid lending anything; it consists of offering everything: "the house and all its contents are at your disposal." You cannot look at a painting, touch a piece of fabric, lift a chair, without someone telling you, with the greatest charm: "It is at your disposal". But beware of accepting even a pin, for it will be an uncouth mistake.

I was guilty of an indiscretion of this kind on my arrival in Palma, and I doubt if I will ever be forgiven by the marquis de... (de la Bastida). I had been well recommended to this young lion of Palma, and I believed that I could accept his offer of a carriage and go for a drive. It had been offered in such a friendly manner! But the next day a note from him made me realise that I had been lacking in good taste, and I hurried to return the vehicle without using it.

I have found exceptions to this rule, but only among people who have travelled, and who, understanding all about the world, really belong to every country. If any of the others had felt obliged to help us, out of the goodness of their hearts, no-one (and it is necessary to point out the inconveniences that customs duties and lack of industry have brought to this rich country), no-one could have given up a corner of their house to us without causing themselves so much inconvenience and hardship, that we would have been very tactless to have accepted their offer.

We recognised their difficulties once we started to look for a place to stay. It was impossible to find a single apartment in the whole town that was fit to live in.

An apartment in Palma consists of four walls, completely bare, without doors or windows. In most of the private houses, they do not use glass; and if one wishes to find this indulgence, which is very necessary in winter, one has to have the frames made. Each occupant, on leaving (and they never leave), takes the windows, the locks and even the hinges with him. His successor begins by replacing them, unless he prefers to live in the open air, which is the usual preference in Palma.

Well, it takes at least six months to have not only the doors and windows made, but also the beds, tables, chairs, everything in fact considering the basic furnishings are so simple and primitive. There are very few workmen; they don't work fast, they lack tools and materials. There is always some reason why the Mallorquin is never in a hurry. Life is so long! One has to be French, which is to say extravagant and frantic, to want anything made straight away. And if you have already waited six months, why not wait another six months? And if you are not happy in this country, why do you stay? Are you needed here? It carries on fine without you. Do you think you can turn everything upside down? Well, you can't. We let you talk, you see, and we do things our own way. - But is there nothing for hire, then? - Hire? What is that? Hire furniture? Is there so much to spare that you can hire it out? - But is there nothing for sale then? - For sale? It would have to be made just the same. Do you think we have time to spare to make furniture in advance? If you want that, have it sent from France, seeing there is everything in that country. - But to order anything from France, we would have to wait six months, more or less, and then pay the import duties. Well then, when one is stupid enough to come here, is the only solution to go back? - That is what I advise you to do, or otherwise have patience, a lot of patience; "mucha calma", that is Mallorquin wisdom.

We were going to take advantage of this advice, when we were offered the bad luck, but certainly with good intention, of discovering a country house for us to rent.

It was a villa belonging to a rich citizen, who for a moderate price, as far as we were concerned, but quite high for this country (around five hundred francs per month), left us his house fully furnished. It was furnished like all Mallorquin country houses. Always camp beds, or wooden ones painted green, some of them made of two trestles on which two planks and a thin mattress were placed; the bare walls whitewashed with lime, and, as an excess of luxury, glass paned windows in nearly all the rooms; finally, in place of tables in the room they call the sitting room, four horrible fire screens in front of the chimney, like those found in our poorest village inns, and which, Señor Gomez, our landlord, had been naive enough to have framed in silk as though they were priceless prints adorning the panelling of his manor house. For the rest, the house was huge, well ventilated (too well ventilated), well laid out, and in a very pleasant situation, at the foot of green, softly rounded mountains, at the far end of a fertile valley which reached the yellow walls of Palma, with the massive cathedral and the sea sparkling on the horizon.

The first few days we spent in this retreat were filled with walks and gentle idleness that suited us in the delightful climate, and the charming countryside which was completely new to us.

I have never been very far from my country, although I have spent a large part of my life on the road. It was therefore the first time that I had seen vegetation and landscape so different from our temperate latitudes. When I first saw Italy, I landed on the beaches of Tuscany and the grandiose ideas I had of that country prevented me from enjoying the beauty of the countryside and its lively charm. On the banks of the river Arno, I imagined that I was on the rivers of India, and I went as far as Venice without being moved or astonished by anything. But in Mallorca, there was nothing I could compare with the places I knew. The people, the houses, the plants, even the simplest cactus on the road, had a distinct character. My children were so struck by it, that they collected everything and tried in vain to fill our suitcases with beautiful quartz stones and veined marbles of all colours, with which the banks of dry stones bordered the fields. Even the peasants, seeing us gathering even dry twigs, either took us to be pharmacists or looked at us frankly as idiots.

CHAPTER SIX

he island owes the great variety of its features to the endless changes brought to its laboured and overworked soil by the disasters of the post primitive area. The area where we were now living, called Establiments, included within the space of a few leagues, very varied landscape.

Around us, all the cultivation, along the fertile slopes, was confined to broad terraces following the contours of the hills. This terraced farming, employed in all parts of the island which the rains and the sudden rise of streams threaten continuously, is very suitable for trees, and gives the countryside the appearance of a well tended orchard.

To the right, hills rose steadily from the sloping pastures to the fir covered mountains. At the foot of these mountains a stream runs in winter and during summer storms, but it was nothing but a bed of stones when we arrived. The lovely mosses that covered the stones, the little bridges, green with the damp, which had cracked with the force of the currents and hidden by branches of willow and poplar, the intertwining of those lovely trees slender and tufted that leaned over to form a cradle of greenery from one bank to the other, a thin trickle of water running silently among the rushes and the myrtles, and always some groups of children, women and goats gathered on these mysterious embankments, made a wonderful scene for a painting. We went for a walk every day along the riverbed and we called this corner of the landscape, *le Poussin*, because its untouched elegance and proud melancholy nature reminded us of the scenes that the great master seems to have particularly loved.

A few hundred steps from our hermitage, the stream divided into several branches and appeared to become lost on the plain. The olive and carob trees spread their branches over the farmland and gave the area the appearance of a forest.

On the numerous hills that surrounded the wooden area, stood stylish cottages, although Lilliputian in size. I don't know how many barns, cart sheds, stables, yards and gardens a farmer can accumulate on an acre of land, and by what natural good taste he unconsciously arranges them. The cottage usually consists of two floors with a flat roof from which the overhanging edge shades an exposed loft, like the row of battlements that rise above a Florentine roof. This level crown creates an air of splendour and strength to the most frail and weak construction and enormous clusters of corn drying in the open air, hang between each opening in the loft, and make a heavy garland alternating in red and amber, and the effect is incredibly rich and attractive. A strong hedge of cactus and prickly pear usually grows around the cottage, and its strange racquet-like leaves entwine like a wall to protect the frail shelters of reed and seaweed that enclose the sheep. As these peasants never rob each other, they need no more to protect their property than a barrier like this. Clumps of almond and orange trees surround the garden, where they grow no other vegetables but peppers and tomatoes, but everything is wonderfully colourful and often, to crown the pretty picture the cottage makes, a single palm tree spreads its graceful parasol or leans gently to one side like a beautiful egret.

This is one of the most flourishing regions of the island, and the reasons M. Grasset de Saint-Sauveur gives in his book, "*Journey to the Balearic Islands*" confirms what I have already said about the general inadequacy of the farming methods used in Mallorca. The observations made by this Imperial Officer in 1807 on the apathy and ignorance of the Mallorquin farmer led him to search for the causes. He discovered two main reasons.

The first was the large number of convents that absorbed a part of the already limited population. These have now disappeared, thanks to M. Mendizábal's forceful decree, for which the devout of Mallorca will never forgive him.

The second is the servile nature that reigns among the Mallorquins and that leads them by the dozen into the service of the rich and well-born. This abuse is still in force. Every Mallorquin aristocrat has a large retinue which his income is barely able to support and which does him no good; it is impossible to be worse served than by this type of honorary servant.

When one wonders how a rich Mallorquin can spend his money in a country with no luxuries or any kind of temptation, it can be explained by looking into their houses at the grubby idlers of both sexes, who occupy a part of the house reserved for them and who, having spent a year in the master's service, have the right to live there for the rest of their lives and to be housed, clothed and fed. Those who wish to retire from service, can do so by giving up these benefits; but custom still allows them to return every morning to take chocolate with their former colleagues and to take part, like Sancho in Gamache's house, in all the festivities of the house.

At first sight, these customs appear to be patriarchal and one is tempted to admire the republican sentiment in the relations between master and servant; but one soon realises that this is closer to the Republicanism of ancient Rome, and that these servants are chained by their laziness or poverty to their master's vanity. It is a luxury in Mallorca to have fifteen servants in the type of house which can support two at the most. When one sees the huge fields lying fallow and industry abandoned, and any thought of progress rejected because of their foolishness and lack of interest, it is difficult to decide which is the most to blame, the master who perpetuates and encourages the moral degradation of his fellow man, or the slave who prefers a degrading idleness to a job that would help him recover his independence and human dignity.

At one time the rich Mallorquin landowners, realising that their expenses were increasing and their revenue was diminishing, decided to improve the efficiency of their tenants and the scarcity of their workers. They sold part of their lands to their peasants, for life, and M. Grasset assures us that, on every large property where this method was tried, the apparently barren earth produced in such abundance, when the men who worked it had an interest in its improvement, that in a few years both parties found that they had benefited from it.

M. Grasset's predictions, in this respect, have been fully realised, and today, the area of Establiments, among others, has become one large garden; the population there has increased, numerous houses have been built on the hills and the peasants have acquired certain comforts which have not yet greatly enlightened them, but which have given them more of an aptitude for work.

It will be many years before the Mallorquin becomes energetic and hard working; and if it is necessary that, like us, he has to pass through the depressing stage of working only for personal gain before he can understand that that is not the aim of humanity, we can leave him to kill the time with his guitar and his rosary. No doubt, a greater destiny than ours is reserved for these infant nations, which we will initiate one day into true civilisation, without them reproaching us for all that we could have done for them. They are not strong enough to survive the storms of revolution that our feelings of superiority have lifted over our heads. Alone, disowned, mocked and attacked by the rest of the world, we have made great strides, and the sounds of our gigantic battles have not yet woken these little nations from their deep sleep, lying in reach of our canon in the bosom of the Mediterranean. A day will come when we baptise them in true freedom and they will come to the feast like workers at the twelfth hour. Let us find the words of our social destiny, let us fulfil our greatest dreams; and as the surrounding nations enter little by little into our revolutionary church, these unfortunate islanders, whose weakness continually exposes them as prey to cruel dominating powers that fight over them, will run to join our communion.

Until the day, when, as first nation of Europe, we can decree a law of equality to all men and of independence to all nations; the law of the strongest army or the most cunning in the game of diplomacy, will rule the world; the right of the people will be nothing but a word, and the only prospect for isolated and restrained nations, *"like the Transylvanian, the Turk and the Hungarian"*, will be to be devoured by a conqueror. If it was always going to be like that, I would not wish Mallorca, either Spain or England or even France as a teacher, and I would take as little interest in the subject of its future as I do in the strange civilisations that we are discovering in Africa.

CHAPTER SEVEN

We had been in Establiments for three weeks when the rains began. Until then we had had wonderful weather; the lemon trees and the myrtles were still in flower, and, during the first days of December, I had stayed outside on the terrace until five o'clock in the morning, enjoying the good fortune of a delightful temperature. You can rely on me, because I don't know anyone on earth who feels the cold like I do, and who is as incapable as I am of ignoring it in order to enjoy the beauties of nature. Moreover, despite the charm of landscape lit by the moon and the perfume of the flowers that rose up to me, my night watch was not very moving. I was not there like a poet in search of inspiration, but as an idler who watched and listened. I was so preoccupied, I remember, with the sounds of the night that I hardly noticed it.

It is true, and everyone knows it, that every country has its sounds, its groans, its cries and its mysterious whisperings, and that this language is by no means the least characteristic feature that strikes a visitor. The strange splashing of the water on the cold marble walls, the heavy measured tread of the '*sbiros*' on the quay, the shrill and almost childlike cries of mice, as they chase each other and quarrel on the slimy flagstones, in fact, every furtive sound that faintly breaks the gloomy silence of the night in Venice, is nothing like the monotonous noise of the sea, or the call of 'Who goes there?' of the watchmen or the melancholy song of the '*serenos*' in Barcelona. The sounds of Lake Maggiore are different from those of Lake Geneva. The continuous crackling of fir cones in a Swiss forest is nothing like the crackling that is heard on a glacier.

In Mallorca, the silence is deeper than anywhere else. The donkeys and mules who spend the night at pasture interrupt it at times by shaking their bells, although the sound is lighter and more melodious than those of the Swiss cows. The sound of a Spanish song rings out in the most deserted places and on the darkest nights. There is not a peasant without a guitar which he carries with him at all times. From my terrace, I could also hear the sea, but so far away and so faint that the strangely fantastic and thrilling poetry of Djins came back to my memory.

J'écoute,	I listen
Tout fuit.	All flees
On doute	We doubt
La nuit	The night
Tout passe;	All passes
L'Espace	Space
efface	Erases
le bruit.	The sound

In the neighbourhood farm, I could hear the crying of a little child, and I could also hear the mother, who was singing him to sleep with a sweet country song, very sad, very Arabic. But other voices far less poetic came to remind me of the grotesque side of Mallorca.

The pigs would wake up and complain in a way that I can't describe. Then the farmer, the father of the family, would be woken by the sound of his darling pigs, just as a mother is woken by the cries of her foster child. I could hear him put his head out of the window and scold the hosts of the stable in a commanding voice. The pigs would understand him perfectly, for they kept quiet. Then the farmer, to get them back to sleep, would start to recite his rosary in a mournful voice which, as his drowsiness came and went, stopped and started like the distant murmur of the waves. From time to time the pigs still let out a wild cry, and the farmer would raise his voice again,

75

without interrupting his prayer, and the docile animals, calmed by an 'Ora pro nobis' or an ' Ave Maria' recited in a certain way, would quiet down immediately. While the child would listen, no doubt, his eyes open, lost in a kind of stupor where unexplained noises plunged the awakening thoughts of man in his cradle, which has such a mysterious effect on him before he can understand.

Then all of once, after such peaceful nights, the deluge began. One morning, after the wind had rocked us all night with its long moaning, while the rain hit against the glass, we heard, as we woke, the sound of a torrent which began to cut a path between the stones of the riverbed. The next day, it sounded louder; the day after that, it washed away the stones in its way. All the blossoms on the trees had fallen off, and the rain poured into the badly shuttered rooms.

We couldn't understand how few precautions the Mallorquins had made against the scourges of wind and rain.

Their delusions and boasts were so great in this respect, that they totally denied that these occasional but serious weather conditions existed. Right up to the end of the two months of downpour we had to endure, they still insisted that it never rained in Mallorca. If we had looked more closely at the peaks of the mountains and the direction of the prevailing winds, we would have been aware in advance of the inevitable hardships that awaited us.

But another disappointment awaited us, one that I mentioned above, when I began by describing my journey by the end. One of our party fell ill. Having a delicate constitution and suffering from a bad sore throat, he soon began to suffer from the damp. The House of the Wind (Son Vent in dialect), which was the name of the villa Señor Gomez had rented to us, became uninhabitable. The walls were so thin that the lime, with which the rooms were plastered, swelled up like a sponge. Never have I suffered so much from the cold, although it was not that cold in reality; to us who were used to keeping warm in the winter, that house, without a fireplace, felt like a mantle of ice over our shoulders, and I was paralysed with cold.

We couldn't get used to the suffocating smell of the braziers, and our invalid began to suffer and to cough.

From that moment we became an object of horror and terror to the population. We were tried and convicted on a charge of pulmonary consumption, which was equivalent to having the plague in the prejudiced view of the Spanish medical profession. A rich doctor who, for the modest fee of 45 francs, deigned to come and visit us, announced however that there was nothing wrong and prescribed no treatment. His main assistant, whom we nicknamed 'Malvavisco' because that was his favourite prescription, was so dirty that our invalid could not bare to let him take his pulse.

Another doctor obligingly came to our rescue; but the pharmacy in Palma was so poorly supplied that we could only buy the most odious drugs. Moreover, the illness must have been aggravated by causes that no science or nursing could treat successfully.

One morning, when we had consigned ourselves to our worst fears over the continuance of the rains and of the suffering that it caused, we received a letter from the severe Señor Gomez to tell us, in the Spanish style, that we were harbouring a person, who was harbouring a disease, that horrified him. That it horrified Don Señor Gomez, no less, the most disgusting ugly man in all the four quarters of the world, that we were bringing disease into his house, and threatening the lives of his family; and for this reason, he was asking us to pack up and vacate his palace in the shortest time possible.

We did not regret this very much, for we could no longer stay there without the fear of drowning in our rooms; but our invalid was in no condition to be moved without danger, especially wit the means of transport available in Mallorca and with the weather that we were having. And then the problem was to know where we could go, because the news of our consumption had spread rapidly, and we could no longer expect to find lodgings anywhere, even at the cost of gold, and even for one night. We were well aware that the kind people, who had offered to help us, were not immune to prejudice themselves, and what's more, that we would be exposing them to the same disapproval as we were experiencing, if they helped us. Without the French consul, who performed miracles in order to gather us all under his roof, we would have been threatened by the possibility of camping in some cave like real Bohemians.

Another miracle occurred. We found ourselves a home for the winter. There was a charterhouse in Valldemossa, where a Spanish refugee had been hiding for, I don't know what, political motive. When we went to visit the charterhouse, we were struck by his distinguished manners, by the melancholy beauty of his wife, and by the simple yet comfortable furnishings of his cell. The poetry of this charterhouse turned my head around. We discovered that the mysterious couple wanted to leave the country in a hurry, and that they were as happy to leave us their furniture and their cell as we were to take it. Thus for the modest sum of a thousand francs, we had a completely furnished dwelling, but one that we could have found in France for a hundred crowns, so rare, costly and hard to assemble were the basic necessities in Mallorca.

We then spent four days in Palma, during which I hardly left the fireplace which the consul had the good luck to own (the deluge still continued). I will now interrupt my narrative to describe briefly the capital of Mallorca. M. Laurens who came to explore and sketch its most beautiful aspects the following year, will be the guide whom I now introduce to the reader, as a more competent archaeologist than I am.

SECOND PART

CHAPTER ONE

lthough Mallorca was occupied by the Moors for four hundred years, few real traces of their occupation survive. In Palma only a small bath house remains.

There is nothing left of the Romans, and as for the Carthaginians only some ruins near their ancient capital of Alcudia and the tradition that Hannibal was born there, which M. Grasset de Saint Sauveur attributes to Mallorquin audacity, although the idea is not entirely improbable.[1]

Yet the Moorish style is preserved in the most basic constructions, and it was necessary for M. Laurens to

(1) The Majorcans claim that Hamilcar, on route from Africa to Catalonia with his wife, already pregnant, stopped at a point on the island where a temple, dedicated to Lucina, had been built, and that Hannibal was born there. The same story can be found in "The History of Majorca" by Dameto. (Grasset de Saint-Sauveur)

correct all the archaeological errors of his predecessors, so that ignorant visitors, like myself, did not think that they had found authentic Arabic remains at every step.

'I have seen no buildings in Palma," wrote M. Laurens, 'that seem very old. The most interesting for their architecture and antiquity all belonged to the beginning of the sixteenth century; but the graceful and splendid art of that period does not take the same form as it does in France.'

'These houses have nothing above the ground floor but one floor and a loft.'[1] The entrance, from the road, consists of a door in a simple arch, without decoration; but its size and the large number of stones radiating out from it, give it an impressive appearance. Daylight enters the large rooms on the first floor through high windows, divided by excessively thin colomns, which give them an entirely Arabic look.'

'This impression was so strong that I had to look at over twenty houses, built in an identical style, and to examine every part of their construction to convince myself that these windows had not been taken from one of those fairytale Moorish palaces of which the Alhambra in Granada remains a fine example.'

(1) These are not exactly lofts but drying rooms, known in the country as porchos.

'I have only seen columns like these in Mallorca, six feet in height and with a diameter of only three inches. The fine quality of the marble of which they are made, the style of the capitals, all led me to assume that they were of Arabic origin. Yet whatever they are, these windows are as beautiful as they are unusual.'

'The loft on the top floor is a gallery or rather a row of windows copied exactly from those which form the crown of La Lonja. An overhanging roof, supported by artistically carved beams, protects this floor from the sun and rain, and produces a pleasant effect of light as it throws long shadows across the house, the brown mass of the woodwork contrasting with the bright tones of the sky.'

'A staircase, made in a grand style, stands in a courtyard at the centre of the house and is separated from the door to the street by an entrance hall, remarkable for its pillars, their capitals carved with leaves or a coat of arms supported by angels.'

'For more than a century after the Renaissance, the Mallorquins continued to build extremely luxurious private houses. While always following the same design, they made changes in the style of the entrance halls and staircases according to architectural fashion. So one finds Tuscan or Doric columns everywhere; ramps, balustrades, always giving the homes of the aristocracy an opulent appearance.'

'This fondness for ornamental staircases and for the Arabic style, is also found in the most humble homes, even when a steep flight of stairs leads straight from the street to the first floor. Each step is decorated with earthenware tiles painted in brilliant blue, yellow and red flowers.'

This description is very accurate and M. Laurens' drawings show the elegance of these interiors very well. These colonnaded court yards would provide a beautifully simple stage design for a theatre set.

The small paved courtyards, sometimes surrounded by columns, like the 'cortile' of the Venetian palace, usually have a simple well in the centre. They look nothing like our empty, dirty courtyards, nor do they serve the same purpose. They never lead to the stables or the coach house. They are genuine inner courtyards, perhaps a reminder of the Roman '*atrium*'. One recognises a kind of '*prothyrum*' and '*cavoedium*'; and the central well oviously replaces the '*impluvium*'.

When these courtyards are decorated with pots of flowers and rushes, they look both elegant and austere, yet the Mallorquin nobility do not understand their poetry, for they cannot help making excuses for the old age of their homes; and if you admire their design, they smile, believing you to be joking, or mistrusting French politeness perhaps as ridicously excessive.

In fact, not everything is equally poetic in the houses of the Mallorquin nobility. There are certain unhygienic aspects which I would be embarrassed to mention to my readers, unless, as Jacquemont said in relation to some of the Indian customs, I wrote in Latin.

Not knowing Latin, I refer those who are curious to a passage written by M. Grasset de Saint--Sauveur, a writer who is not as serious as M. Laurens but very truthful in this respect, devoted to the larders in Mallorca and in many old houses in Spain and Italy. This passage is remarkable if only for the medical prescription he mentions,, which is still used in Mallorca and which is very strange indeed. (See Grasset de Saint Sauveur, page 119).

The interior of these palaces does not correspond in any way to the exterior. Nothing is more revealing than the arrangement and furnishing of a room to the character of a nation or an individual.

In Paris, where changes in fashion and abundance of manufactured goods create such a strange variety of styles in a home, it is only necessary, is it not, to walk into someone's house, to get an idea of their character, in a wink of an eye, to know if they have good taste and good ideas, to know if they are greedy or lazy, methodical or romantic, hospitable or ostentatious.

I have my own system of judgement, like everyone else, which doesn't prevent me from being wrong sometimes and being right in others.

I have a particular horror of barely furnished and very tidy rooms. Unless they have such intelligence and good heart that they are completely beyond any material considerations and only live there as if they were in a tent, I imagine the owner of such a home to have an empty head and a cold heart.

I cannot understand how anyone can live between four walls and not want to decorate them, if only with logs and baskets, or have something alive around, if only a potted wallflower or a poor sparrow.

Emptiness and stillness make me cold with dread, rigid order and symmetry break my heart with sadness, and if I could imagine eternal damnation, my idea of hell would certainly be to live forever in some provincial house where perfect order reigns, where nothing ever changes place, where nothing can ce seen lying about, where nothing is ever worn our or broken, and where no animal is allowed to enter, on the pretext that animated objects damage inanimate one. Ah! Let all the carpets in the world burn, if I am only allowed to enjoy them on condition that no child, dog or cat is ever seen playing on them.

This rigid tidiness does not come from a true love of tidiness but from excessive laziness or a sordid sense of economy. With a bit more care and effort, a sympathetic housekeeper of my choice, can keep the rooms in our house in a state of tidiness, which I cannot live without either.

But what can one say or think of the habits and ideas of a family whose 'home' is empty and silent, without the excuse or the pretext of tidiness?

Although one can easily be mistaken, as I said earlier, in an individual case, it is more difficult to be mistaken in a general sense. The character of a nation is revealed by their clothes and by their furnishings as much as by their customs and their language. Having been all over Palma looking at apartments, I entered a large number of houses; all of them are so alike that I can conclude from them the general character of their occupants. I did not enter any of these interiors without my heart growing heavy with annoyance and boredom, just at the sight of their bare walls, their marked and dusty flagstones, the odd, dirty furniture. All bore witness to indifference and inactivity, never a book, never a lady's needlework. The men don't read, the women don't even sew. The only sign of domestic activity is the smell of garlic that betrays the act of cooking, and the only sign of private amusement are cigar butts squashed on the paving.

The absence of intellectual life turns a room into something dead and empty, which has no comparison among us, and which makes the Mallorquin resemble an African more than a European.

Therefore all these houses where the generations have succeeded one another without ever changing anything round, and without making any individual contributions to the things that normally form part of our lives, give more an impression of caravans than of real houses. While ours give the impression of a family nest, theirs resemble huts where groups of a wandering population can retire casually to spend the night. People who know Spain well, have told me that it is generally the same all over the Peninsula.

As I said earlier, the courtyards or atriums in the palaces of these Mallorquin knights (which is still the way the countrymen of Mallorca are addressed) have an air of hospitality and even comfort. But once you have climbed the elegant staircase and entered the rooms, you could easily believe that you had entered a place devoted entirely to sleep,. These vast halls, usually in the form of a long rectangle, very high, very cold, very dark, completely bare, white washed without any decoration, with huge old family portraits, completely black and arranged in a single row, so high up that nothing can be distinguished; four or five chairs of rough, worm-eaten leather, edged with big gilded nails which haven't been polished for a hundred years; a few Valencian mats or merely some long-haired sheepskins thrown here and there on the paving stones; casement windows placed high up in the walls and covered with heavy curtains; large doors of black oak like the beams in the ceilings and sometimes an ancient door curtain of gold brocade, richly embroidered with the family coat of arms, but tarnished and mildewed with age: that is what the Mallorquinn palaces are like inside. No other tables are to be seen except dining tables; mirrors are very rare and take up so little space in their enormous frames, that they throw hardly any light.

The master of the house can be found standing, smoking in deep silence, the mistress seated on a large chair, playing with her fan, without a thought in her head. One never sees the children: they live in the kitchen with the servants or in the attic, for all I know; the parents do not bother with them. A chaplain comes and goes around the house, but does nothing. The twenty or thirty manservants take their siesta, while one old, flustered maid opens the door after the visitor has rung the bell fifteen times.

This way of life certainly does not lack character, as we would say, with the unlimited meanings we give to the word nowadays; but if the most placid of our French citizens was condemned to live like this, he would certainly go crazy with despair, or rebel from spiritual depression.

CHAPTER TWO

he three most important buildings in Palma are the Cathedral, La Lonja (the Exchange) and the Royal Palace.

The Cathedral, which the Mallorquins attribute to King Jaime the Conqueror, their first Christian king and in a way their Charlemagne, was in fact begun during his reign, but was not completed until 1601. It is immensely bare and built entirely from finely grained limestone of a beautiful amber colour.

This impressive pile, which stands on the edge of the sea, makes a great impression on the visitor as he enters the harbour; but it has nothing of any real value or good taste, except for the southern portal,, which M. Laurens describes as the most beautiful example of Gothic art he had ever had the chance of drawing. The interior is extremely austere and dark.

Because the sea winds blow through the large ope-

nings in the main doorway with such fury and over-
turn pictures and sacred vessels during the service,
they have walled up the doors and the rose windows on that side. The nave is at least five hundred
and forty palms[1] long and three hundred and
seventy-five wide.

In the middle of the chancel is a simple marble sar-
cophagus which is opened for visitors to show them
the mummified body of Jaime II, son of the
Conqueror, a devout prince who was as weak and
gentle as his father was adventurous and warlike.

The Mallorquins consider their Cathedral far superior to that of Barcelona, just as their Lonja is infinitely more beautiful, according to them, than the one in
Valencia. I cannot verify this or support the first opinion.

In both these cathedrals, as in most Spanish cities,
one notices a peculiar trophy that adorns the end of
the organ pedentive. It is a hideous Moor's head of
painted wood, wearing a turban. This severed wooden head is often adorned with a long white beard
and painted red underneath to represent the impure
blood of the defeated.

(1)
*The Spanish 'palmo' is equivalent to the 'pan' of our cen-
tral provinces)*

On the keystones of the arches above the nave can be seen numerous coats of arms. To have one's coat of arms displayed in the house of God was a privilege for which the Mallorquin nobles paid heavily; and it was thanks to this investment to vanity that the Cathedral could be finished in a century when Catholic devotion had cooled. It would be unfair to accuse only the Mallorquins of a weakness that was common to all devout noblemen in the world at that time.

La Lonja is the building that impressed me the most, with its elegant proportions and an originality that manages to include perfect symmetry and simplicity in very good taste.

This Exchange was begun and completed in the first half of the fifteenth century. The illustrious Jovellanos described it in detail and the 'Magasin Pittoresque' made it popular by publishing a very interesting drawing several years ago. The interior is one vast room, supported by six slender pillars, fluted in spirals.

Originally intended as a meeting place for merchants and the numerous seamen that flocked to Palma, La Lonja bares witness to the past splendour of Mallorquin commerce; it is only used these days for public festivals. It would have been interesting to see the Mallorquins, dressed in the rich costumes of

95

their fathers, solemnly amusing themselves in this ancient ballroom, but the rain kept us captive in the mountains and it was not possible for us to see the carnival, which is not as well known or as sad, perhaps, as the one in Venice. As far as La Lonja is concerned, however beautiful it appeared to me, it has not erased from my memory that adorable jewel, called La Cadoro, the ancient Mint on the Grand Canal.

The Royal Palace of Palma, which M. Grasset de Saint-Sauveur does not hesitate to call Roman and Moorish (this inspired in him emotions completely in keeping with the Empire), is said to have been built in 1309. M. Laurens declares that his conscience is troubled by the position of the small, twin windows and the mysterious little columns that he examined in the building.

Would it be too daring to ascribe all the anomalies in style found in Mallorquin buildings to the inclusion of ancient fragments into subsequent buildings? Just as in France and Italy, the Renaissance style included medallions and bas-reliefs in their sculpture that were really Greek and Roman. Isn't it equally probable that the Mallorquin Christians, after tearing down all the Moorish buildings[1], made use of those

(1) *The capture and sacking of Palma by the Christians in December 1229 is vividly described in the 'Chronicle of Marsili (unpublished). Here is an extract.'the plunderers and thieves ransacking the houses found beautiful Moorish women and charming young girls holding gold and silver coins, pearls and*

valuable remains to decorate their own, later constructions?

Whatever else it is, the Royal Palace of Palma looks very picturesque. Nothing could be more unsymmetrical, more inconvenient and more savagely mediaeval, more proud, more individual and more noble than this manor house, composed of galleries, towers, terraces and arcades, clinging to each other at a considerable height and topped by a Gothic angel who, from the bosom of the clouds, looks towards Spain across the sea.

This palace, which holds the archives, is the residence of the Captain General, the most important person on the island. Here is how M. Grasset de Saint-Saveur describes the interior of the house:

precious stones, gold and silver bracelets, sapphires and all kinds of precious jewels in their laps. They displayed all these before the eyes of the armed men in front of them and, crying bitterly, said to them in Saracen: 'All this is for you, but just give us enough to live on.'

The lust for gain was so strong, their behaviour so bad, that the men of the King of Aragon's household did not appear before him for eight days, so engrossed were they in searching for hidden treasure to rob.

It reached such a state that the next day, unable to find the cook or the king's house servants, an Aragonese noblement called Ladro said to him:

'Sire, I invite you to be my guest because I have more than enough to eat and they tell me that I have a good cow in my quarters; you can have a meal and sleep there tonight.'

the king was deligthed and followed the nobleman.

'The first room is a sort of hall used as a guardroom. One turns right through two large rooms where hardly a chair can be found.

'The third room is an audience hall; it is furnished with a red velvet throne, fringed with gold and standing on a platform, up three carpeted stairs. On either side stands a lion of gilded wood. The canopy that covers the throne is also of crimson velvet, surmounted by a plume of ostrich feathers. Above the throne hang portraits of the King and Queen.'

'It is in this room that the General receives on ceremonial and gala occasions representatives from the various branches of civil administration, officers of the garrison and important visitors.'

The Captain General, acting in the role of Governor, to whom we had brought letters of introduction, did in fact do us the honour of receiving one of our party in this room, when he brought the letters to him. Our companion found this important officer close to his throne, the same one, I am sure, that Grasset de Saint-Sauveur described in 1807; for it was worn, faded, threadbare and stained with oil and candle wax. The two lions were no longer gilded, but they still made fierce grimaces. Only the royal effigy had changed; this time it was the innocent Isabella who, like a monstrous advertisement for cabaret,

occupied the old, gilt frame, where her venerable ancestors had succeeded each other, like models on an art student's canvas. Despite being housed like Hoffman's Duque d'Ireneus, the Governor was a very respected man and a very courteous prince.

The fourth building worth mentioning is the Town Hall; a sixteenth century building which can be compared with good reason to the style of the palaces in Florence. The roof is particularly remarkable for its projecting eaves, like those of Florentine palaces and Swiss chalets; but it is unusual in that it has supporting wooden caissons, richly carved with rosettes, alternating with long caryatids resting on the beams which they seem to hold up unwillingly, for most of them have their faces hidden in their hands.

I have not seen the interior of this building, in which can be found a collection of portraits of the great men of Mallorca. Among them the famous Don Jaime can be seen, portrayed as the King of Diamonds. There is also a very old painting of the funeral of the Mallorquin, Ramon Llull, which presents a very interesting and varied array of old costumes, worn by people in the procession to honour the illustrious doctor. Finally, there is a magnificient painting of Saint Sebastian by Van Dyck in this municipal building, which no-one in Mallorca bothered to mention to me.

'Palma has a school of art,' adds M. Laurens, 'which has already produced, in our nineteenth century alone, thirty-six painters, eight sculptors, eleven architects and six engravers, all celebrated professors, if we are to believe the 'Dictionary of Celebrated Mallorquin Artists', recently published by the learned Antonio Furio. I must admit that during my stay in Palma I never realised that I was surrounded by so many great men, for I never saw anything to give me any idea of their existence...'

'Some of the rich families have paintings from the Spanish School ... But if you search the shops, if you enter the homes of the ordinary people, you will find nothing but those coloured prints that are sold by pedlars in our public market places, and which are only to be found in France beneath the humble roof of the poorest peasant.'

Palma is particularly proud of the Palace of the Count of Montenegro, now an old man in his eighties, formerly the Captain General, and one of the most illustrious figures in Mallorca, by birth but more importantly for his wealth.

This gentleman has a library which we were allowed to visit, but where I did not open a single book and of which I would have said absolutely nothing (my respect for books being equal to terror), if a learned friend had not told me of the priceless treasures

I had passed by unknowingly, like the cock in the fable among the pearls.

This Frenchman, M. Tastu.[1], spent nearly two years in Catalonia and Mallorca, studying the Ro-mance language, and he kindly lent me his notes and allowed me, which is rare among scholars, to use them as I liked. I will not do so without warning my reader beforehand that this traveller was as enthusiastic about everything in Mallorca as I was disappointed.

I can explain the difference in our impressions by the fact that during my visit the Mallorquin population was disturbed and confined to make room for twenty thousand Spanish refugees from the war and that it may not have been by mistake or prejudice that I found Palma less habitable and the Mallorquins less willing to welcome another group of foreigners than they had been, no doubt, two years earlier. But I would rather incur the blame of a benevolent critic than write under any other impression than my own.

I would be very happy, however, to be contradicted and corrected in public, as I have been in private, for the public would gain a far more exact and interesting book on Mallorca that this disconnected and perhaps, unjust account, that I am forced to give them.

So let M. Tastu publish his travels; I will read with

[1] *One of our most erudite linguists, and married to one of our most talented and noble muses.*

heartfelt joy, I swear, anything that can change my opinion of the Mallorquins: I have met several whom I would like to consider representative of a general type and who, I hope, will not doubt my feelings for them, should this book ever fall into their hands.

I find then, in M. Tastu's notes on the intellectual wealth that Mallorca still possesses, this library belonging to the Count of Montenegro, that I hurried through so irreverently behind the private chaplain, concerned that I had to examine the home of an old, aristocratic, Mallorquin bachelor; a sad, sombre home, if ever there was one, ruled over by a silent priest.

'This library,' says M. Tastu, 'was formed by the uncle of the present Count Montenegro, the Cardinal Antonio Despuig, intimate friend of Pope Pius VI.'

'The learned Cardinal collected everything of bibliographical repute that Spain, Italy and France had to offer. The section dealing with numismatology and ancient art is especially complete.

'Among a small number of manuscripts to be found there, is a curiosity for lovers of calligraphy: a Book of Hours. The miniatures are exquisite; and it belongs to one of the best periods in mediaeval art.

'Lovers of heraldry will find an Armorial there in

which the coats of arms of the Spanish nobility are shown with their colours, including the families of Aragon, Mallorca, Roussillon and Languedoc. The manuscript, which appears to be from the sixteenth century, belonged to the Dameto family, who are connected to the Despuig and the Montenegros. Looking through it, we found the coat of arms of the Bonapart family, the ancestors of our great Napoleon, and so we tore out the page on order to examine it later...'

'A beautiful nautical chart can still be found in this library, handwritten by the Mallorquin Valesqua in 1439, a work of art in calligraphy and topographical drawing, on which the miniaturist has also added his precious work. The chart once belonged to Amerigo Vespucci, who paid a high price for it, according to an inscription written on the back at the time: 'Questa ampla pelle di geographia fu pagata da Amerigo Vespucci CXXX ducati di oro di marco.' (This large geographical chart was paid for by Amerigo Vespucci 130 ducats in gold coin.)

'This valuable monument to mediaeval geography will soon be published as a supplement to the Catalan-Majorcan Atlas of 1375, included in Volume XIV, Part 2, of the Notes on Manuscripts of the Academy of Inscriptions and Letters.'

As I copy out this note, my hair stands up on my head, as a dreadful scene comes to my mind.

We were in this library and the chaplain was unrolling this very chart in front of us, this precious and rare treasure, bought by Amerigo Vespucci for 130 gold ducats, and God knows how much the antiquarian Cardinal Despuig paid for it! ... When one of the forty or fifty servants thought of putting a cork inkstand on one of the corners of the parchment to keep it open on the table. The inkstand was full, but filled to the brim!

The parchment, used to being rolled up, and pushed at that moment perhaps by some evil spirit, moved, cracked, lifted and curled up on itself dragging the inkstand, which emptied onto the rolled chart, overcoming all restraint. There was a general cry of horror; the chaplain became paler than the parchment.

The chart was slowly unrolled, still believing in some vain hope! Alas! The inkstand was empty! The Chart had been flooded, and the pretty little kings painted in miniature were literally floating on a sea, blacker than the Black Sea.

Then everyone lost his head. I think the chaplain fainted. The servants ran about with buckets of water, as if there had been a fire, and tried to clean the chart with great swoops of the sponge and the scrubbing brush, haphazardly sweeping away kings, seas, islands and continents.

Before we could stop this fatal enthusiasm, the chart was partly destroyed, but not irretrievably spoiled. M. Tastu had traced it exactly, and thanks to him, it will be possible to more or less repair the damage.

But what must have been the chaplain's dismay when his master found out about it! We were all standing six paces from the table at the moment of the catastrophe, but I am certain that we will take all the blame and that the accident, attributed to the French, will not put them back into the good books of the Mallorquins.

This tragic event prevented us from admiring or even noticing the rest of the marvels in the Montenegro Palace, neither the cabinet of medals, nor the antique bronzes, nor the paintings. We were anxious to leave before the Count returned, and certain that we would be accused in front of him, we didn't dare to return there. M. Tastu's notes will have to cover once again for my ignorance.

'Adjoining the Cardinal's library, a cabinet of medals can be found, a priceless collection of Celtic-Iberian, Moorish, Greek, Roman and mediaeval medals, which are at present in an unbelievable mess and require an expert to arrange and classify them.'

'The rooms of Count Montenegro's Palace are

decorated with ancient marble and bronze statues, either from the excavations at Aricia, or bought in Rome by the Cardinal. There are also many paintings of the Spanish and Italian schools, many of which would dazzle the most beautiful galleries in Europe.'

I must also mention the Castle of Belver or Bellver, the ancient residence of the Mallorquin Kings, although I only saw it from a distance, on the hill where it majestically overlooks the sea. It is a very old fortress, and one of the strongest state prisons in Spain.

'The walls that survive today,' writes M. Laurens, 'were built at the end of the thirteenth century and are still in a good state of conservation. It is one of the most curious mediaeval military buildings.'

When our traveller visited it, he found about fifty Carlist prisoners there, covered in rags and half naked, some of them only children, eating from a large pot of coarse, boiled macaroni, with an infectious gaiety. They were guarded by soldiers, who knitted their socks, with a cigar in their mouths.

It was the Castle of Bellver, at that time, that took the overflow from the prisons in Barcelona. But more important prisoners have been locked behind these formidable doors.

Don Gaspar de Jovellanos, one of the most gifted orators and the most forceful writers in Spain paid the price here for his famous pamphlet 'Bread and Bulls'. He was imprisoned in the 'Tower of Homage, whose dungeon,' says Vargas, 'is the most brutal of prisons.' Jovellanos spent his dreary leisure writing a scientific description of the castle, and an account of the tragic events that took place there during the wars of the Middle Ages.

The Mallorquins also owe to his visit on their island, an excellent description of the Cathedral and La Lonja. In a word, his 'Letters on Mallorca' are the best documents that can be found.

The same dungeon that Jovellanos occupied in the reign of the parasitic Prince of Peace, was occupied soon afterwards by another scientist and political celebrity.

This little known fact in the life of a man as well known in France as Jovellanos is in Spain, is interesting only because it is one of the romantic chapters in a life in which a love for science would throw him into a thousand dangerous and moving adventures.

CHAPTER THREE

ommissioned by Napoleon to measure the Meridian, M. Arago was in Majorca in 1808 on a mountain known as L'Esclop de Galatzó[1], when he heard the news of the events in Madrid and the abduction of Ferdinand.

The inhabitants of Majorca were so infuriated by the news that they decided to capture the French scholar and set off in a crowd towards the L'Esclop de Galatzo to kill him.

(1) George Sand mentions this mountain on three occasions, which she calls 'Leclop de Galatzo', not 'Le Clot' as it is incorrectly written in the first edition of 'Un Hiver A Majorque' (Hyppolyte Souverain, Paris 1842), an error which has been repeated in every successive edition.

George Sand should have written, in good Majorquin, 'Esclop', but 'Leclop' sounds as if it refers to the mountain itself, whereas 'Clot' means an excavation or a hole.

We can find the correct and incorrect versions in the original manuscript, preserved in the Cell Museum at the Charterhouse in Valldemossa. Editor.)

This mountain is situated on the coast where Jaime 1st landed when he came to capture the island from the Moors; and as M. Arago often lit a fire there for warmth, the Mallorquins imagined that he was signalling to a French squadron, carrying an army landing party.

One of the islanders, called Damian, quartermaster of the brig attached by the Spanish Government to the scientific expedition to measure the Meridian, decided to warn M. Arago of the danger he was in. He ran ahead of his compatriots and arrived in good time with a sailor's suit as a disguise.

M. Arago left his mountain immediately and returned to Palma. He came across the men on the way, who were going to tear him to pieces, and they asked him for news of the accursed 'Gabacho' whom they wanted to kill. Speaking the local language fluently, M. Arago answered all their questions without being recognised.

Arriving in Palma, he reached the brig; but the captain, Don Manuel de Vacaro, who had always followed his orders until then, formally refused to take him to Barcelona and would only hide him on board in a crate that proved too small to fit M. Arago.

A next day, a threatening mob had gathered on the quay, and Captain Vacaro warned M. Arago that he could no longer answer for his life, adding, on the advice of the Captain General, that his only hope of safety was to hand himself over as a prisoner to the Castle of Bellver. They provided him with a launch to cross the harbour. The people saw him and rushed in pursuit, and were about to catch him at the moment when the doors of the fortress closed behind him.

M. Arago spent two months in that prison, until the Captain General at last assured him that he would turn a blind eye to his escape. He did escape, with the help of M. Rodriguez, his Spanish associate in the measuring of the Meridian.

The same Mallorquin, Damian, who had saved his life on the L'Esclop de Galatzo, took him to Algiers in a fishing boat, having refused at any price to land in France or Spain.

During his captivity, M. Arago learned from the Swiss soldiers who were guarding him, that certain monks on the island had offered them money if they would poison him.

In Africa, our scholar had many other adventures, from which he made an even more miraculous escape; but this is not part of our subject, and we hope that one day he will write down this interesting story.

At the first sight, the Mallorquin capital does not reveal its true character. It is only when one explores in the evening, penetrating deep into its mysterious streets, that one is struck by the elegant style and original design of even the simplest buildings. But it is, most of all, from the North, when one approaches the city from the interior, that it presents its most African features.

M. Laurens was aware of its picturesque beauty, which would not have struck a normal archeologist, and he sketched one of the views that particularly impressed me with its grandeur and melancholy; it was a section of the wall near the Church of Saint Augustine, where a huge square tower stands with no other opening but a small, arched doorway.

A stand of beautiful palm trees crowns the building, the remains of a Templar fortress, which stands in the foreground, wonderfully sad and sparse against a magnificient view which stretches from the foot of the ramparts across a fertile plain to the distant, blue mountains of Valldemossa. Towards the evening, the colours of the landscape change from hour to hour, becoming more and more harmonious; we have seen a sparkling pink at sunset, turn to splendid violet, and then to silvery lilac, and finally to pure, tranparent blue as night falls.

M. Laurens drew several other views from the walls of Palma.

'Every evening,' he says, 'at the hour when the sun colours objects so vividly, I would walk slowly along the wall, stopping at every step to look at the delightful compositions made by the arrangement of outlines of the mountains and the sea with the tops of buildings in the city.'

'Here, the embankment below the walls was covered by a terrifying hedge of aloes, sprouting hundreds of tall branches with flowering heads that look so much like a monumental candelabra. Beyond this, clumps of palm trees rose above the gardens, amidst the fig trees, cacti, orange trees and rubber trees; further away appeared the covered roof terraces shaded with vines: and at last, the spires of the Cathedral, the bell towers and domes of numerous churches that stood out in silhouette against the clear and luminous background of the sky.'

Another walk that M. Laurens enjoyed as much as I did, was among the ruins of the Convent of Saint Dominic.

At the end of a vine pergola, supported by marble pillars, were four large palm trees which rose from the height of a terraced garden and appeared gigantic. At that height, their tops were on a level with the highest buildings in the city. Through their branches could be seen the top of the facade of Saint Etienne, the massive tower of the famous Balearic clock [1] and the Angel Tower on the Royal Palace.

The Convent of the Inquisition, which is no more than a mound of rubble, where only a few scrubs and aromatic herbs grow here and there among the ruins, did not fall by the hand of time. A far more

(1) This clock, which has been described at length by the two greatest Mallorquin historians, Dameto and Mut, still worked thirty years ago, and this is what M. Grasset de Saint Saveur said about it: 'This very ancient machine is called 'The Sun Clock'. It marks the hours from sunrise to sunset, following the understood larger or smaller daily and nocturnal arcs, so that on the 10th of June it will sound the first hour of the day at five-thirty and the fourteenth hour at six-thirty in the evening, the first hour of the night at eight-thirty and the nineth at four-thirty the following morning. On the 10th of December the process is reversed. Throughout the year the hours are accurately regulated, according to the variation in the rising and setting of the sun. The clock is not very useful to the local people, who tell the time by modern clocks; but it helps to remind gardeners when to water their gardens. No-one knows from where or when this machine was brought to Palma; presumably it didn't come from Spain, France, Germany or Italy, where the Romans had introduced the practice of dividing the day into twelve hours, beginning at sunrise.

According to a churchman, the Rector of Palma University, in the third part of his work on the Sephardic religion, Jewish refugees at the time of Vespasian took this famous clock from the ruins of Jerusalem and brought it to Mallorca where they had found refuge. Here you have a marvellous origin, in keeping with the characteristic partially of our Islanders for anything sensational.

The historian Dameto and consequently Mut placed the age of the Baleraric Clock in the year 1385. It was bought by the Dominican fathers and placed in the tower where it still exists.' ("Voyage aux îles Baleares et Pithuises", 1807. Grasset de Saint-Sauveur.)

rapid and unrelenting hand, the hand of revolution, pulled it down and almost ground it to dust. Only a few years ago, this building was said to have been a work of art, and even the remains, the fragments of rich mosaic and the slender arches still standing in the void like skeletons, testify at least to its magnificence.

The destruction of these sanctuaries of Catholic art in all of Spain is a subject of great indignation among the Palma nobilty and a source of legitimate regret among artists. Ten years ago, perhaps even I would have been more shocked by the violence of this destruction than by the page of history that it illustrates.

Although there is good reason to deplore the weak and yet violent measures needed to carry out the decree, as M. Marliani does in his 'Political History of Modern Spain', I swear that as I stood in the middle of these ruins I felt an emotion that was not the sadness that ruins normally inspire. A thunderbolt had fallen there, and a thunderbolt is a blind instrument, a brutal force like the anger of man; but the law of providence that rules the elements and their apparent disorder, knows very well that the beginnings of new life are hidden in the ashes of destruction. On the day when the convents fell, there was something in the political atmosphere in Spain similar to nature's need for renewal through fruitful convulsions.

I cannot believe what I was told in Palma, that a few malcontents avid with vengeance and greed, performed this act of violence in front of an outraged population. It requires a lot of malcontents to reduce an enourmous building to dust, and it would require a very unfeeling population to stand and watch the decree carried out, if they felt so strongly against it.

I would rather believe that as the first stone was dislodged from the top of the dome, the feelings of belief and repect also fell from the soul of the people, held there no more firmly than the monks' bell tower to its base; and that each one, feeling a sudden urge in their guts, threw themselves on the corpse with a mixture of courage and horror, of fury and remorse. The monatic system protected much abuse and flattered much egoism. Religion is very powerful in Spain and no doubt more than one destroyer repented the next day to the monk whom he had chased from hi s sanctuary. But there exists in the hearts of the most ignorant and blind of men something that makes hm tremble with excitement when destiny offers him a special mission.

The Spanish people had built these arrogant palaces for their ordinary clergy with their own money and sweat and they came to the door for centuries to receive the farthing of idle supplication and the bread of mental slavery. They had taken part in their crimes, they had bathed in their cowardise. They had built up the pyres of the Inquisition. They had been accomplices and informers in atrocious persecutions against entire races, whom they wished to eradicate from their midst. And when they had accomplished the ruin of the Jews, who had enriched them, when they had banished the Moors, to whom they owed their civilization and their greatness, they were punished by heaven with poverty and ignorance. They were determined and pious enough not to blame the clergy, their creation, corruptor and scourge. They suffered instead, for a long time, bent beneath the aoke of their own making. And then one day strange, audacious voices came to their ears and into their minds with words of liberation and deliverance. They understood the error of their ancestors, blushed at their humiliation, felt indignant at their poverty, and despite the idolatry they still felt towards icons and relics, they broke the images, and believed more strongly in their rights than in their cult.

What then is the secret power that can change a prostrate believer, all at once, to the point where he can turn his fanaticism in a single day against the objects he has adored all his life? It is certainly neither dissatisfaction with man, nor boredom with objects. It is a dissatisfaction with himself, it is boredom with his own weakness.

The Spanish people were greater on that day than one would think. They accomplished a decisive act, and removed for themselves the means of going back on their decision, like a child, who, wanting to become a man, breaks his toys so that he can no longer be tempted to return to them.

As for Don Juan Mendizábal (his name deserves to be mentioned in this context), if what I have understood about his political life is reliable, he was a man of principle rather than action, and in my opinion, that is the best praise that one could give him. That this statesman overrated the intellectual capacity of Spain at one time and doubted it at others, that he took inadequate and untimely measures sometimes, and sowed his ideas on barren land where the seeds were choked and eaten, that is perhaps a good enough reason to deny him the practical ability and persistence needed for the immediate success of his plans; but that is no reason why history, taken from a more philosophical point of view than usual, will not hail him one day as one of the most generous and ardently progressive minds[1] in Spain.

(1) This correct thinking, this elevated idea of history inspired M. Marliani to praise M. Mendizábal at the beginning of his criticism of the government: ...'One can never deny him those qualities, which are even more admirable as they are rarely found among the men who preceeded him to power: It is a lively faith in the future of the country, it is an unlimited devotion to the cause of liberty, it is a passionate belief in the nation, an honest enthusiasm for progressive and even revolutionary ideas, to make reforms which the state of Spain cried our for; it is a great tolerance, a great generosity towards his enemies; it is in the end a total disinterest in personal

These thoughts often returned to me among the ruins of the Mallorquin convents, when I heard his name attacked and it was not perhaps convenient for us to praise and sympathise with him. I told myself however that despite the political questions of the day, of which I admit I have neither a liking nor a knowledge, I can still form a sympathetic judgement of men and even events without fear of embarrassing myself. it is not as important as one believes or one says to know a country firsthand, as to study its customs and material conditions in depth, in order to get a real idea of its history and its possibilites, in other words, its spiritual life. It seems to me that the whole history of mankind follows a long line, which

gain, which caused him to sacrifice his own interests at all times and on all occasions to the interests of his country, and which went so far as to leave him, at the close of his various ministries, without a single ribbon in his buttonhole ... He is the first minister to have taken the revival of his country seriously. His term of office marked real progress.
this time the minister spoke the language of a patriot. he did not have the power to abolish censorship, but he was generous enough to free the Press from all restrictions, which favoured his enemies against him. He submitted his administration to the free examination of public opinion and when a violent opposition rose against him within the Parliament, formed by his former allies, he was noble enough to respect the rights of the deputy, whom he had once heaped with honours and who had become his most ardent political enemy. M. Mendizábal's noble example is all the more praiseworthy for having no precedent! Nor has he found himself any followers in this virtuous policy of tolerance!' (The political History of Modern Spain' by M Marliani)

is the same for all nations and to which the threads of each private history is attached. This line is the awareness and perpetual striving towards the ideal, or if you like, towards perfection, which man carries with him, either in a state of blind instinct, or in a state of enlightened theory. Really brilliant men have all felt this and tried more or less in their own way to achieve it, and the strongest, those who have had the most lucid ideas and have caused the greatest changes at the time to hasten the development of the future, have always been condemned by their contemporaries. They have been dishonoured and condemned without being known, and it is only when the fruits of their labours have been collected, that they have been placed on a pedestal, until some transistory deception, some misunderstood setback has forced them to descend.

How many famous names in our Revolution have belatedly and timidly been revived! And how badly understood and badly developed, their work and their mission! In Spain, Mendizábal was one of the most severely judged of all their ministers, because he was the bravest, the only brave one perhaps; and the act that made his short term in power unforgettable, the destruction of the monasteries, was the one for which he has been so harshly criticised, that I feel I have to protest here in favour of that audacious decision and the delirious enthusiasm with which the Spanish people adopted it and put it into practice.

At least, that was the feeling that suddenly filled my heart at the sight of those ruins, not yet blackened by time, which also seemed to be protesting against the past and to be proclaiming the return of truth among the people. I do not think that I have lost a taste or a respect for the arts, I do not feel that I have an instinct for vengeance or barbaric acts; in fact I am not among those who say that the cult of beauty is useless, and that historic buildings should be destroyed to make way for factories; but a monastery of the Inquisition torn down by the hand of the people is also a great page in history, as instructive and as moving as a Roman aqueduct or an amphitheatre. A government administration that orders in cold blood the destruction of a temple, for whatever useful or ridiculous economic reason, would be committing a disgraceful and crimininal act; but a political leader who, in a decisive and dangerous day, sacrifices art and science for more precious gains, reason, justice, religious freedom, and a nation who, despite their pious instincts, their love for Catholic pomp and their respect for the clergy, find enough heart and strength to execute a decree, in the wink of an eye, are like sailors in a storm who save themselves by throwing their valuables into the sea.

Cry then, those who will over the ruins! Almost all these buildings, whose destruction we deplore, are the dungeons in which either the soul, or the body of humanity has languished for centuries. Then the poets arrive, who, instead of deploring the passing of the world's infancy, celebrate in their verses about fragments of golden playthings and blood stained canes, the virile age that the world has thrown away! Beautiful verses have been written by Chamisso about his ancestral home, destroyed in the French Revolution. His poem ends with a thought that is very new in poetry, as well as in politics.

Blessed art thou, old manor,
over whom the plough now passes!
and blessed is he,
who drives the plough over you!

After recalling the memory of that beautiful poem, do I dare to write a few pages, inspired by the Dominican monastery? Why not, since the reader must also be indulgent when it comes to judging a thought that the writer has sacrificed her self respect and her old tendencies to offer him? May this fragment, such as it is, throw a bit of variety on the dry list of buildings that I have just completed!

CHAPTER FOUR

THE MONASTERY OF THE INQUISITION

midst the rubble of a ruined monastery, two men met in the clear light of the moon. One appeared to be in the prime of life, the other bent beneath the weight of years. He was however the younger of the two.

They both trembled when they found themselves face to face; for the night was advanced, the road deserted and the Cathedral clock tolled the hour slowly and mournfully.

The one who appeared to be old was the first to speak:

'Whoever you are, man,' he said, 'you have nothing to fear from me. I am weak and broken down. Don't expect anything from me either, for I am poor and naked upon the earth.'

'Friend,' answered the young man, 'I am only hostile to those who attack me and, like you, I am too poor to fear robbers.'

'Brother,' replied the man with worn features, 'then why did you tremble when I approached?'

'Because I am a bit superstitious, like all artists, and because I took you to be the ghost of one of those monks who are no longer here and whose broken graves we are treading on. And you, friend, why did you also shake when I approached?'

'Because I am very superstitious, like all monks, and because I took you to be the ghost of one of those monks who buried me alive in the grave you are treading on.'

'What did you say? Are you really one of the men for whom I have eagerly searched the land of Spain in vain?'

'You will no longer find us anywhere in the daylight; but in the darkness of the night, you can still find us. Now your waiting is fulfilled. What do you want with a monk?'

'Look at him and question him, my father. Engrave his features on my memory, in order to reproduce him in paint. Collect his words, in order to repeat them to my countrymen. Finally, to get to know him, to understand what is mysterious and poetic and great about a monk and the life in a cloister.'

'Where do you come from, traveller? What a strange idea you have of things? Don't you come from a country where the Papal rule is abolished, the monks outlawed and the cloisters suppressed?'

'There are still religious souls among us in favour of the past, and imaginations struck by the poetry of the Middle Ages. Anything than can give us a faint scent, we look for, we cherish and we adore almost. Ah! Don't believe, father, that we are all blind desecrators. We artists, we hate the brutal people who soil and break everything they touch. Far from approving of their orders of death and destruction, we attempt in our pictures, in our poetry and our plays, in fact in all our works to revive the old traditions and renew the spirit of mysticism which gives birth to Christian art, that perfect child!'

'What are you saying, son? Is it possible that the artists of your free and prosperous country can be inspired by anything other than the present? There are so many new things to sing about, to paint and to celebrate! Yet according to you they are bent to the ground where their ancestors lie sleeping? They search in the dust of graves for a living, virile inspiration, while God in his goodness has given them such a sweet and beautiful life?'

'I cannot believe, good monk, what you must think our life is like. We artists do not concern ourselves with politics and social questions interest us even less. We search in vain to find any poetry in the things going on around us. The arts are declining, inspiration is smothered, bad taste triumphs, men are occupied with material things and if we didn't have the cult of the past and the monuments of previous centuries to inspire us, we would lose the sacred fire altogether, which we guard with such effort.'

'I have been told that human genius has never carried the science of happiness so far as in your country, nor the marvels of industry, nor the advantages of freedom. Have I been misinformed then?'

'If you were told, father, that material riches have never given us so much luxury, so much comfort and by destroying the old society, such a horrifying variety of tastes, opinions and beliefs, then you have been told the truth. But unless you were told that all these things, instead of making us happy, have debased and degraded us, you were not told the whole truth.'

'How can such a strange thing have happened? All the reasons for happiness become poison on your lips, and everything that made man great and just and good, comfort and freedom has made small and miserable? How do you explain this contradiction?'

'Father, do I have to remind you that man does not live by bread alone? Because we have lost our faith, nothing we have acquired since, can benefit our souls.'

'Explain to me again, son, how you could have lost your faith, since religious persecution has ceased in your country, you have been able to enlarge your souls and lift your eyes to the divine light? That was the moment to believe, since it was the moment to understand. So, at that moment, did you doubt? What cloud could have passed over your heads?'

'A cloud of weakness and human misery. For isn't investigation incompatible with faith, father?'

'It is as if you were asking, young man, if faith is compatible with truth! Don't you believe in anything then, my son? Or else you believe in a lie.'

'Alas! I only believe in Art. But isn't that enough to give the soul strength and confidence and sublime joy?'

'As far as I know, my son, and I don't really understand it. Are there still some happy men among you then? And you, are you safe from defeat and sorrow.'

'No, father, artists are the most unhappy, the most angry and tormented of men; as they see the object of their worship fall lower every day and their efforts are powerless to elevate it.'

'How can it be that such dedicated men let the arts perish instead of reviving them`?'

'Because they no longer have any faith and without faith, art is no longer possible.'

'Didn't you just say that for you art is a religion? You contradict yourself, my son, I cannot understand you.'

'And how can we avoid contradicting ourselves, father! God has given us a mission and the world denies it, the present has closed the gates on us to glory and inspiration and life; we are forced to live in the past, and ask the dead the secrets of eternal beauty, because men of today have lost their religion and overturned their altars?"

'We are filled with stength and enthusiasm in front of the works of the great masters and as long as the hope of equalling them still exists, but when we try to achieve our ambitious dreams and an unbelieving and narrow minded world blows a cold wind of disdain and insult over us, we can produce nothing that conforms to our ideal and the thought dies in our breast before it can come to light.'

The young artist spoke with bitterness, the moon lit his sad, brave face, and the silent monk watched him in naive and kindly surprise.

'Let us sit down here,' said the latter, after a moment of silence, stopping beside the massive balustrade of a terrace, that overlooked the town, the countryside and the sea.

It was at an angle to the garden of the Dominicans, that not long before had been rich in flowers, fountains and precious marbles and that now was strewn with rubble and invaded by all the tall weeds that grow with such speed and vigour among ruins.

The traveller, agitated, crushed one of them in his hand and threw it away with a cry of pain. The monk smiled.

'That prick is sharp,' he said, 'but not at all dangerous. My son, that bramble you carelessly grasped and that hurt you, is symbolic of those coarse men that you complained about earlier. They invade the palaces and monasteries.... They climb on the altars and occupy the ruins of the ancients marvels of the world. Look with what vigour and strength these foolish weeds have filled the flowerbeds where we grew our precious, delicate plants so carefully, yet not one of them has survived our neglect! In the same way, simple, half savage men who were thrown away like useless weeds, have reasserted their rights and choked the poisonous plant which grew in the shade and was called the Inquisition.'

'Couldn't they have choked it without destroying the sanctuaries of Christian art and the works of genius at the same time?'

'That detestable plant had to be pulled out, because it was hardy and rampant. These cloisters had to be destroyed right to the foundations where the root was hidden.'

'Well father, what is beautiful or good about these thorny weeds that grow in their place?'

The monk thought for a moment and then replied:

'As you tell me you are a painter, presumably you will make a drawing of these ruins?'

'Certainly. What are you getting at?'

'Will you avoid drawing these great brambles that hang in festoons over the rubble and swing in the wind, or will you be happy to include them in your composition, as I have seen in a picture by Salvator Rosa?'

'They are an inseparable part of the ruins and no painter would fail to include them.'

'Then they too have their beauty and significance and therefore their use.'

'Your parable is no longer true, father; sit a few beggars and gypsies down among the ruins and they will only make them more sinister and desolate. The painting would gain from it, but what would humanity gain?'

'A beautiful picture, perhaps, and certainly a good lesson. But you artists, who give us this lesson, do not understand what you are doing, you only see the stones that have fallen and the weed that have grown.'

'You are being hard; I could reply that you who talk like this only see your prison broken down and your freedom recovered by this catastrophe; because I suspect, father, that the monastery was not to your liking.'

'And you, my son, could you love art and poetry enough to live here without regret?'

'I imagine that it would have been the most beautiful life in the world for me. Oh! What a vast and noble monastery this must have been! What splen-

dour and elegance these remains suggest! How pleasant it must have been to come here in the evenings
and breathe the soft air and dream to the sound of
the sea, when these airy galleries were paved with
rich mosaics, when crystal clear water murmured in
marble basins and a silver lamp shone like a pale star
in the heart of the sanctuary! What deep peace, what
majestic silence you must have enjoyed, when the
respect and confidence of your people surrounded
you like an impregnable wall and they crossed themselves and lowered their voices every time they passed in front of your mysterious doorways! Ah, who
wouldn't like to renounce all the worries, all the con-
cerns and ambitions of social life to come and bury
themselves here in peace, oblivious to the whole
world, on condition that they remain here as artist
and devote ten even twenty years to a single painting, which would be polished slowly, like a precious
diamond, and be seen placed on an altar, not to be
judged and criticised by the first ignorant soul but
hailed and invoked as an image worthy of the Deity
itself!'

'Stranger,' said the monk severely, 'your words are
full of pride and your dreams are nothing but vanity.
In this art that you talk about with such emphasis and
exalt so highly, you only see yourself, and the isola-
tion you long for, is only in your eyes a means of
making yourself great and godly. I can understand
now how you can believe in this selfish art without

believing in any religion or society. But perhaps you did not consider these things in your mind before you spoke; perhaps you are ignoring what has happened in these caverns of corruption and terror. Come with me, and perhaps what I am going to show you will change your feelings and your ideas.'

Across the mountains of rubble and unsteady, crumbling heaps, the monk led the young traveller, not without danger, to the centre of the ruined monastery; and there, in the part where the prisons had been, he made him descend carefully along a wall of solid masonry, fourteen feet thick, which pick and shovel had split along its depth. At the heart of this terrible crypt of stone and cement, like gaping jaws in the heart of the earth, opened cells, without air or daylight, separated from each other by stone blocks as thick as those that weighed down the gloomy roof.

'Young man,' said the monk, 'these pits that you see are not wells or even tombs, they are the cells of the Inquisition. It is here that for centuries men have been left to die slowly, whether guilty or innocent before God, whether debased by vice, whether misled by passion, or inspired by genius and virtue, they dared to have ideas that differed from those of the Inquisition.'

These Dominican fathers were scholars, men of

letters, even artists. They had huge libraries where theological subtilities, bound in gold and watered silk, rested on ebony shelves, their spines shining with pearls and rubies. While man, that living book where God has written down His thoughts in his own hand, they buried alive and kept hidden in the bowels of the earth. They had engraved silver vases, chalices glittering with precious stones, magnificient pictures and gold and ivory madonnas, while man, that chosen vessel, that chalice filled with heavenly grace, that living image of God, they abandoned alive in the coldness of death and to the worms of the tomb. So many of them could grow roses and snow-drops with as much care and love as one gives to a growing child, yet they could watch without pity as their fellow man, their brother, faded and rotted in the dampness of the tomb.

That is what it means to be monk, my son, that is what the cloister is like. Brutal savagery on one hand, cowardly fear on the other; selfish intelligence or gut-less devotion, that is the Inquisition.

And when these foul vaults were opened to the light of the heavens, if the hand of the liberators disturbed a few columns and tarnished a few gilded images, should the tomb stones be replaced over the dying victims, should we cry over the fate of their torturers, because they were deprived of their gold and their slaves?'

The artist had descended into one of the vaults to examine the walls. For a moment he tried to imagine the struggle that the human will, buried alive, would sustain against the dreadful despair of such captivity. But no sooner had his lively and impressionable imagination tried to paint this picture, than he was filled with anxiety and terror. He thought he could feel the icy vaults weighing on his soul, his limbs trembled, his lungs gasped for air, he felt faint with the desire to leap out of the abyss, and stretching his arms towards the monk, who had remained at the entrance, he cried out:

'Help me, father, in Heaven's name, help me to get out of here!'

'Well, my son,' said the monk as he offered him a hand, 'what you experience now at the sight of bright stars over your head, imagine what I felt when I saw the sun after ten years of the same torture!'

'You, unhappy monk!' cried the traveller, hurrying towards the garden, 'how could you stand ten years of this living death without losing your mind or your life? It seems to me that if I had stayed there a moment longer, I would have gone crazy or raving mad. No, I didn't think that the sight of a dungeon could produce such sudden and profound terror, and I cannot understand how the mind could adapt to it or accept it. I have seen the instruments of torture in

Venice, I have also seen the dungeons of the Ducal Palace and the dark passage where the victims fell, struck by an unseen hand, and the flagstones, pierced with holes, where the blood dripped into the waters of the canal without leaving a trace. I only thought then about death being more or less rapid. But in the dungeon that I have just left, it is the terrifying idea of living there that worries me. Oh my God! To be kept there and not allowed to die!'

'Look at me, my son,' said the monk, uncovering his bald and wrinkled head, 'I have lived no longer than you with your masculine face and your smooth brow, and yet you took me no doubt to be an old man.

How much I deserved my slow agony and how I endured it, doesn't matter. I am not asking for your pity; I no longer need it, I feel so happy and young nowadays, at the sight of these ruined walls and empty cells. Nor do I want to inspire in you a horror of the monks. They are free and so am I. God is good to everyone. But as you are an artist, it is good that you have known one of the emotions, without which an artist cannot understand his work.'

'And now, if you want to paint these ruins, where you came just now to cry over the past and where I come every night to bow down and give thanks to God for the present, your hand and your talent will perhaps be inspired by a higher thought than easy regret or dumb admiration. Many buildings, which might be priceless objects to an historian, have no other value than to remind us of the human actions put into building them and these are often wicked and childish. Since you have travelled, you will have seen the bridge in Genoa with gigantic piers thrown across a chasm and the sumptuous and solid church, built at great expense in a deserted place by a vain aristocrat, because he wouldn't cross the water and kneel in the church with the local people. You may also have seen the pyramids in Egypt which stand as an appalling testiment to the slavery of nations or those dolmens over which human blood ran in torrents to satisfy the insatiable thirst of barbaric gods. But you artists don't usually consider the reason behind the works of man, only the beauty and originality of their execution. Therefore your intellect often loves the outward execution of an idea that your heart would reject if it was conscious of it.

This is why your own work often lacks the true colours of life, especially when you force yourself to copy lifelessly from the work of the dead, which you don't want to understand, instead of expressing the feelings that course through the veins of living men.'

'Father,' replied the young man, 'I understand your lessons and I certainly won't ignore them; but do you really believe that art can be inspired by such a philosophy? You explain, with the wisdom of our age, something that was conceived by our fathers in a poetic delirium of naivety and superstition. If, instead of the happy gods of Greece, we were to expose the banal allegories hidden beneath their voluptuous forms, if instead of the divine Florentine madonna, we were to comb in the Dutch style, a sturdy servant from a coffee house; and finally if we gave Jesus, the Son of God, a naive philosophy from the school of Plato; instead of gods we would have nothing but men, just as here, instead of a Christian temple, we have nothing in front of us but a heap of stones.'

'My son,' said the monk, 'if the Florentines gave the Virgin her divine traits, it is because they still believed in her; and if the Dutch gave her common features, it is because they no longer believe in her. You flatter yourself that you can paint sacred subjects nowadays, when you only believe in art, in other words, in yourself! You will never succeed. So try to record only what is palpable and alive for you.'

'If I myself had been a painter, I would have made a beautiful picture devoted to recording the day I was freed; I would have shown the strong, bold men, a hammer in one hand and a torch in the other, forcing their way into the limbo of the Inquisition, which I have just shown you, and bringing from the stinking dungeon, dull eyed ghosts, with frightened smiles. One could have seen, like a halo on all their heads, the light of the heavens falling over them from a crack in the broken roof, and it would have been a subject as beautiful and as appropriate to my time as the Last Judgment of Michelangelo was to his; for these simple people who seem so coarse and dispicable to you in their destructive actions, seem more beautiful and noble to me than all the angels of heaven. Just as this ruin which strikes you as an object of sadness and consternation, seems to me a far more religious monument that it ever was before its destruction.

If I was asked to erect an altar as a witness to future ages of the grandeur and power of ours, I would want none other than this mountain of rubble, over which I would write this on the sacred stone:

'In the time of ignorance and cruelty, men worshipped the God of vengeance and punishment at this altar. On the day of justice and in the name of humanity, men overturned these blood stained altars, hated by the God of mercy.

CHAPTER FIVE

It was not in Palma but in Barcelona, in the ruins of the house of the Inquisition, that I saw those dungeons cut from massive stones, fourteen feet thick. It is quite possible that there were no longer any prisoners left in the monastery in Palma when the people entered it. It would be a good idea to ask the susceptible Mallorquins to allow me 'poetic licence' for the piece you have just read.

All the same, I have to say, as nothing is invented without a certain basis of truth, that I met a priest in Mallorca, now the rector of a Palma parish, who spent seven years of his life, 'the flower of his youth', in the prisons of the Inquisition, and who could only leave under the protection of a lady who had taken a special interest in saving him. He was a man in the prime of life, with very lively eyes and a cheerful manner. He didn't appear to miss the rules of Holy Office very much.

As for the Dominican monastery, I will quote a passage from Grasset de Saint-Sauveur, who cannot be accused of bias, since he had previously written a pompous oration in praise of the Inquisitors, with whom he had been in contact in Mallorca:

'One still sees paintings in the cloister of Saint Dominic that recall the barbaric acts once committed against the Jews. Each of the unfortunate men, who were burned, is portrayed in a picture and underneath their name, age, and date of death have been written.

'I was told that, a few years ago, the descendants of these unfortunate men who now form a particular class among the inhabitants of Palma, known by the ridiculous name of 'Chouettes', tried in vain to get these distressing records removed, by offering quite considerable sums of money. I refuse to believe this story.'

'I will never forget however the day that I was walking in the Dominican cloister and thinking painfully about these sad pictures, when a monk approached me and showed me several among them marked with cross-bones:

'These,' he said, 'are the portraits of those whose ashes were exhumed and thrown to the wind.'

'My blood froze; I left quickly, my heart broken and my spirit shocked by the scene.'

'By chance, a book printed in 1755 by the order of the Inquisition fell into my hands. It contained the names, surnames, occupations and offences of the unfortunate victims sentenced in Mallorca between 1645 and 1691.'

'I trembled as I read this account; there I discovered that four Mallorquins, including a woman, had been burned alive for Judaism; thirty-two others died for the same reason in the dungeons of the Inquisition and their bodies were burned; three were then dug up and their ashes thrown to the wind; a Dutchman accused for Lutheranism, a Mallorquin of Moham-medanism, six Portuguese, including a woman, and seven Mallorquins believed to be Jews, burned in effigy, having had the good luck to escape. I counted two hundred and sixteen other victims, Mallorquins and foreigners, accused of Judaism, heresy and Mohammedanism taken from prison, after publicly recanting their faith and returned to the bosom of the Church.

This ghastly list closed with a decree by the Inquisition which was no less terrible.

M. Grasset then gives the Spanish text, so here is an exact translation:

143

"All the accused, mentioned in this account, were publicly condemned by the Holy Office as official heretics; all their possessions were confiscated and given to the Royal Treasury; they were declared unqualified and incapable of work, neither eligible to receive any titles or benefits, ecclesiastic or secular, nor any public honnor or position. They were not allowed to carry on their person, or allow their dependants to carry either gold or silver, pearls, precious stones, coral, silk, camlet or fine cloth, nor allowed to ride a horse, nor carry arms, nor use anything that, by common law, Royal decrees or laws, instructions or rules of the Holy Office, was prohibited to individuals thus degraded; the same prohibition extended for women condemned to the fire, to their sons and daughters, and for the men, even to their grandsons in the male line, condemning at the same time, the memory of those burned in effigy, ordaining that their bones (when they could be distinguished from those of faithful Christians) be exhumed, returned to justice and the secular courts, to be burned and reduced to ashes. All inscriptions found on the graves would be removed or scraped off, whether affixed or painted, however they were placed, in a way 'that nothing remained of them on the face of the earth but the memory of their sentence and their execution.'

When one reads such documents, so close to our own time, and when one sees the relentless hatred that still exists in Mallorca today towards this unfortunate race even after twelve to fifteen generations of Jews converted to Christianity, one cannot believe that the spirit of the Inquisition has died out as completely as they claim at the time of Mendizábal's decree.

I will not finish this chapter, or leave the Monastery of the Inquisition, without telling my readers of a very curious discovery, which I owe completely to M. Tastu. It would have made his fortune, thirty years ago, at least if he had not taken it, with a happy heart, to the Master of the World, without bothering to keep a part for himself, which is more likely what he would have done, considering his untroubled and disinterested artistic character.

This exert is too interesting for me to attempt to cut it. So there it is, exactly as it was put into my hands, with permission to publish it.

MONASTERY OF SAINT DOMINIC IN PALMA, MALLORCA

A companian of Saint Dominic, Miguel de Fabra, founded the Order of preaching friars in Mallorca. He came from Old Castilla and accompanied Jaime I in the conquest of the Great Balear in 1229. His knowledge was great and varied, his devotion remarkable, which gave him a strong hold over the Conqueror, his nobles and even over the soldiers.. He preached to the troops, held divine services, gave holy communion to his helpers and fought the infidels, as the clergy did at that time. The Arabs claimed that the Blessed Virgin and Father Miguel alone defeated them. It was said that the Aragonese and Catalan soldiers would pray, after God and the Holy Virgin, to Father Miguel Fabra.

The famous Dominican father had received the habit of his order in Toulouse from the hands of his friend Dominic: He was sent by him to Paris, with two other companions, to accomplish an important mission there. It was he who established the first Dominican monastery in Palma, through a donation he received from the Bursar of the first Bishop of Mallorca, D.J.R. de Torella: This happened in the year 1231.

A Mosque and a few adjoining plots of land served as the first foundation. Later, the preaching brothers enlarged the community by a profitable trade in all kinds of merchandise, and by the freqent donations given by the faithful. Meanwhile, one of the founders, the brother of Miguel Fabra, had gone to die in Valencia, which he had helped to conquer.

Jaime Fabra was the architect of the Dominican monastery. It does not say whether he belonged to the family of Father Miguel, his namesake, we only know that he handed in his plans around 1296, for

11

he later draw up the plans for the Cathedral in Barcelona (1317) and then others in the lands of the King of Aragon.

The monastery and its church must have gone through many changes in the course of time, if one compares for a moment, as we have done, the different parts of the ruined building by appearance. Here is a fine doorway only just standing, in the style of the fourteenth century; but further on, forming part of the building, are broken arches, whose heavy keystones lying among the rubble indicate that architects other than Jaime Fabra and very inferior to him have been at work here.

Over these vast ruins, where nothing was still standing except for a few century palms, which we begged them to save, we could lament, as we did over the monasteries of Santa Catalina and San Francisco in Barcelona, that the cold hand of politics alone had been responsible for these indiscriminate acts of destruction.

In fact, art and history have lost nothing by the fall of San Jeronimo in Palma or San Francisco, which obstructed the sea wall in Barcelona; but in the name of history and in the name of art why couldn't they have saved the monastery of Santa Catalina in Barcelona and Saint Dominic in Palma, as historic monuments, where the naves sheltered the tombs of good people, 'las sepulturas de personas de be', as it said in the little notebook we held in our hands, which came from the monastery archives? There one finds after the name of N. Cotoner, Grand Master of Malta, the names Dameto, Muntaner, Villalonga, La Romana and Bonapart!

This book, together with everything that remains of the monastery, now belongs to the contractor who demolished it.

This man, a typical Mallorquin, who at first startles you, but then charms and reassures you, noticing our interest in the ruins and their history and, moreover, like all men of the people, a great admirer of Napoleon, eagerly showed us a tomb adorned with the arms of Bonapart, his forefathers, according to Mallorquin tradition. We found this curious enough to do some research on the subject; but occupied with other work, we were unable to give the time or the attention necessary to complete it.

We discovered the coat of arms of the Bonaparts, which are:

'Parti per pale azure and gules: in the first, six mullets or, displayed by two, two and two: on the second, a lion leopardy or: on an chief or: an eagle sable.'

1. In an Armigery or book of heraldry, which formed part of the valuable contents of the Count of Montenegro's library, we made a copy of this coat of arms.

2. In Barcelona, in another Spanish armigery, not as beautifully made, which belonged to a learned archivist from the Court of Aragon, we found proofs of nobility, dated 15th June 1549, of the Fortuny family, under which appears, among the four quarters, the maternal grandmother, who came from the house of Bonapart.

In this register: Index: Pedro III, volume II of the archives of the Crown of Aragon, can be found two acts, dating from 1276, relating to members of the 'Bonapar' family. This name, of Provencal or Languedoc origin, underwent Mallorquin alterations, like so many others of the era, and would have become Bonapart.

In 1411, Hugo Bonapart, a native of Mallorca, went to the island of Corsica as 'Regent' or governor to King Martin of Aragon; and it is to him that the origin of Bonaparte can be traced, or as they were later called Buonaparte, therefore Bonapart is the Roman name, Bonaparte is old Italian, and Buonaparte modern Italian. We know that members of Napoleon's family signed themselves either Bonaparte or Buonaparte.

Who can say what difference these slight discoveries might have made a few years earlier, if they had helped to show Napoleon, who held so much importance to being French, that his family came originally from France?

Without the same political importance, M. Tastu's discovery is no less interesting today and if I had a say in the distribution of government funds destined for the Arts, I would provide this bibliographer with the means of completing his research.

It is of little importance today, I agree, to prove the French origin of Napoleon. This great captain, but in my view (and I apologise to present fashion) not such a great prince, who by nature was certainly a great man, was able to adapt so well to France. Posterity will not care whether his ancestors were Florentine, Corsican, Mallorquin or from Languedoc, but history will always be interested in lifting the vale obscuring this elect race, of which Napoleon was certainly not just a happy accident or an isolated case. I am sure that, if one looked carefully, one would find men and women in the previous generations of that family, who were worthy of such a descendant, and here the coat of arms, the hereditary insignia, of which the Law of Equality has done justice, but which the historian must always remember could well throw some light on the warlike and ambitious destiny of previous Bonaparts.

When, in fact, has a shield been as proud and as significant as this one belonging to the Mallorquin knights? This lion in the position of attack, this sky covered with stars, where the prophetic eagle is trying to break away, isn't it a mysterious sign of a very unusual destiny? Napoleon, who loved the poetry of the stars with an almost superstitious enthusiasm and who made the eagle the emblem of France, could he have known about his Mallorquin shield, and unable to find the origin, assumed the Provencal 'Bonpar' and kept quiet about his Spanish ancestors? It is the fate of great men, after their death, to watch as nations argue over their cradles or their graves.

PROVAS DE PERA FORTUNY A 13 DE JUNY DE 1549
Proofs of Nobility of Pera Fortuny on 13th June 1549

FORTUNY

His father, of the ancient noble house of Mallorca.

Field of silver, five black roundels, two, two, one

COS

His mother, of the ancient noble house of Mallorca

Filed of gules (red), a bear of gold, crowned with a fleur-de-lys of the same colour.

BONAPART

His paternal grandmother, of the ancient noble House of Mallorca.

Here the description of the shield is missing: the dissimilarities result from the fact that whoever painted this nobiliary, was not aware of what he was copying; what's more it is inaccurate.

GARI

His maternal grandmother, of an ancient noble house of Mallorca.

Quartered in gules (red) and silver, three silver towers, two and one, and three wavy bands of silver.

BONAPART

Obtained from an armorial manuscript containing the coat of arms of the principal Mallorquin families, etc., etc.
The manuscript belonged to D. Juan Dameto, the Mallorquin chronicler, who died in 1633, and is kept in the library of the Count of Montenegro. It is a sixteenth century manuscript.
Mallorca, 20th September 1837
M. Tastu

PART THREE

CHAPTER ONE

We left for Valldemossa around mid December on a clear morning and took possession of our charterhouse on one of those beautiful sunlit autumn days which were to become more and more unusual for us. After crossing the fertile plains of Establiments, we reached that indeterminate terrain, sometimes wooded, sometimes dry and stony, sometimes damp and cool, but always changing abruptly, which resembled nowhere else.

Nowhere, except in a few valleys in the Pyrenees, has nature appeared to me as free as on these heathlands of Mallorca, such open spaces, that created a certain sense of confusion in my mind with the Mallorquin's claim to have put all their territory under perfect cultivation.

I would not dream however of reproaching them, for nothing is more beautiful than these neglected lands that produce whatever they wish and that have need of nothing: tortured trees, bent and dishevelled; terrible brambles, magnificent flowers, carpets of moss and reeds, spiky caper bushes, delicate and charming lilies; and everything growing in the way God wished it, ravine, hill, stony path falling suddenly into a field, a green road sinking into a hollow brook, a prairie open to all corners, that soon ends at the foot of a mountain peak; then undergrowth strewn with huge boulders which one would think had fallen from the sky, roads running deep beside a stream between myrtle bushes and honeysuckle; finally a farm thrown like an oasis into the heart of this wasteland, lifting its palm tree like a lookout to guide the traveller in the wilderness.

Neither Switzerland nor the Tyrol could have given me this impression of free and primeval creation that delighted me so much in Mallorca. It seemed to me that even in the wildest Swiss mountains, nature exposed to such rugged weather conditions has escaped the hand of man only to be restrained even more harshly by the sky and to overcome this, like a passionate soul freed from itself, is enslaved by its own mutilations.

In Mallorca, she flourishes under the kisses of a blazing sky, and smiles under the attack of mild squalls that sweep over her as they cross the seas. The reclining flower rises again with more strength, the fallen trunk grows a greater number of shoots after the storm; and as there are, to tell the truth, no really empty spaces on this island, the absence of well-made roads gives it an air of abandon or of revolt, which must bare a resemblance to those wonderful savannahs of Louisiana where, in the cherished dreams of my childhood, I followed Rene in search of traces of Atala or of Chactas.

I am sure that my praise of Mallorca will not please the Mallorquins, for they consider that they have very pleasant roads. Pleasant to look at, I don't deny, but practical for carriages, you will have to judge for yourself.

The local carriage for hire is a "tartane", a type of old fashioned omnibus, drawn by a horse or a mule, and without springs of any sort; or a "birlocho", a type of open cab which seats four, that rests on its shafts like the tartane, as it is blessed with solid wheels and massive iron fittings, and the interior is padded with six inches of wool stuffing. Such deep padding certainly gives you good reason for a moment's thought the first time you sit down in this vehicle with such a luxurious appearance! The driver sits on a plank, which serves as a seat, his feet straddling the shafts and the horse's rump between his legs, so that he has the advantage of feeling, not only all the jolts of his barrow, but also every movement of his beast, and to be thus riding on the coach and on the horse at the same time. He doesn't appear to be unhappy with this method of travel in the least, for he sings all the time, despite the frightful shaking he receives, and only interrupts his song to swear dreadfully at his horse, when the poor animal hesitates to throw itself down some precipice or to climb some wall of rocks.

For this is the way one travels: ravines, streams, bogs, live hedges, ditches obstruct the way in vain; one does not stop for so little. All this, what's more, calls itself the road.

On leaving, you decide on the route with the driver, as a bet in bad taste, and you ask your guide if a fly has bitten him.

'It's the road,' he tells you. 'But this river?' 'It's the road.' 'And this deep hole?' 'The road,' 'And this thicket as well?' 'Still the road.' - 'Good luck!'

Then you have nothing more to do but take your place, bless the upholstery of the interior without which you would undoubtedly have had broken limbs, commit your soul to God, and contemplate the scenery in anticipation of death or a miracle.

And yet you sometimes arrive safe and sound, thanks to the steadiness of the carriage, the strength of the horse's legs and even perhaps to the indifference of the driver, who does not interfere, but crosses his arms and peacefully smokes his cigar, despite the fact that one wheel runs on a mountain and the other in a ravine.

One adapts very quickly to danger when one sees that others take no notice of it: even though the danger is real enough. It does not always turn over, but when it does, it seldom can be righted. M. Tastu experienced an accident like this the year before on our route from Establiments, and he was left for dead where he lay. He kept having terrible headaches, which did not however dampen his desire to return to Mallorca.

Almost all the people have some sort of vehicle and the nobility have those carriages from the time of Louis XIV, with a widened box, some with eight windows, and with enormous wheels that can brave all obstacles. Four or six strong mules can easily pull these heavy machines, with bad suspension, pompous and ungainly, but spacious and strong, in which one crosses the most terrifying passes at a gallop with incredible daring, but not without some bruises, bumps on the head or at least terrible stiffness.

The sober Miguel de Vargas, a truly Spanish author, who never makes a joke about anything, talks about the 'horrorosos caminos' (horrifying roads) of Mallorca in these terms:

'One cannot emphasize strongly enough the neglect of this essential branch of administration on this Balearic Island. What they call a road is a string of impassable obstructions, and the route from Palma to the mountains of Galatzo presents the unfortunate traveller with death at every step,' etc.

On the outskirts of the towns, the roads are a little less dangerous, but they have the serious disadvantage of being closed between two walls or two ditches, which will not let two vehicles pass. In the worst situation, the oxen have to be unhitched from the cart or the horses from the carriage and one of the two vehicles has to reverse, often for a long distance. Then there are interminable discussions to decide who will give way; and during this time, the traveller, already late, has nothing more to do but repeat the Mallorquin motto: mucha calma' for his own edification.

With so little money spent on the upkeep of their roads, the Mallorquins have the advantages of having plenty of them. They have, if anything, too great a choice. I have only taken the route between the Charterhouse and Palma three times, and back again: six times I have followed a different route and six times the 'birlocho' has lost its way and made us wander up hill and down dale, under the pretext of searching for a seventh road which we were told was the best of all, and which was never found.

From Palma to Valldemosa, measures three leagues, but three Mallorquin leagues, which cannot be covered at the fast trot in less than three hours. One rises without realising it for the first two leagues; on the third, one reaches the mountains and follows a very level ramp (originally the work of the monks, apparently), but very narrow, horribly rapid, and more dangerous than all the rest of the road.

Here, one begins to approach the Alpine side of Mallorca; but although the mountains rise on either side of the gorge, although the torrent leaps from rock to rock; it is only in the depth of winter that these places take on the wild appearance that the Mallorquins attribute to them. In the month of December, despite recent rains, the torrent was still a charming rivulet running between tufts of grass and flowers; the mountain was cheerful and the enclosed valley of Valldemosa opened before us like a garden in Spring.

To reach the Charterhouse, it was necessary to alight from the carriage, for no vehicle can climb the paved road that leads to it, a road delightful to the eye for its daring progress, winding between beautiful trees, and the enchanting views that appear at every step, becoming more beautiful the higher one climbs. I have seen nothing more pleasing, and yet more melancholy at the same time, than these views of green oak, carab, pine, olive, poplar and cypress combining their varied shades in deep pools, veritable depths of greenery, where the stream follows its course through thickets of lavish richness with inimitable grace. I will never forget a certain turn in the gorge where, turning around, one can distinguish one of those pretty, little Arabic houses, which I have described, on the top of a hill, half hidden by cactus leaves and a large palm tree leaning across the void, silhouetted against the air. When the sight of mud and fog in Paris makes me miserable, I close my eyes and see again, as if in a dream, that green mountain, those fawn coloured rocks, and that solitary palm tree lost in a pink sky.

The Valldemosa range rises from plateau to plateau closed in to a narrow kind of pass, surrounded by high mountains and shut off to the North by the slope of a final plateau where the monastery stands at the entrance. The Carthusian monks have softened the ruggedness of this romantic place, with an enormous amount of work. They have made a vast garden out of the valley at the end of the mountain range, enclosed by walls that do not spoil the view at all, and bordered by triangular cypress trees, planted in pairs on various levels, that give it the ordered look of a cemetery at the Opera.

The garden, planted with palms and almonds, occupies the sloping end of the valley and rises in large tiers up the first part of the mountain. In the moonlight, when the uneven tiers are shrouded in shadow, it appears to be an amphitheatre fitted for the battles of giants. In the centre, under of group of beautiful palm trees, a stone reservoir collects the water from mountain springs and carries it in stone canals to the terraces below, just like the ones that irrigate the surrounding countryside of Barcelona. These canals in Mallorca as in Catalonia, are too numerous and too ingenious to be anything but the work of the Arabs.

The Charterhouse stands on the last level of this pass in the mountains and faces north over a spacious valley which widens and rises, sloping gently towards the coastal cliffs, where the sea pounds and corrodes at the base. One branch of the mountain range stretches towards Spain and the other to the east. Therefore the picturesque Charterhouse dominates the sea on both sides. So one can hear it thunder to the north and see it as a faint shimmering line over the mountains that descend to the immense plain which unfolds to the south: a beautiful picture, framed in the foreground by black rocks covered with fir trees, beyond that, by the rugged profile of the mountains, fringed with wonderful trees, then by rounded peaks which the setting sun gilds in warm colours and over which the eye can distinguish, a league away, tiny silhouettes of trees as thin as a butterfly's antennae and as black as a pen stroke of Chinese ink, upon the glittering gold background.

This shining background is the plain, and at that distance, when the mountain mist begins to rise and throws a transparent veil over the chasm, one could believe that it was already the sea. But the sea is even further away, and when the sun returns and the plain resembles a blue lake, the Mediterranean makes a bright, silver band on the edge of that wonderful sight.

It is one of those views which is overwhelming because it leaves nothing to desire and nothing to the imagination. Everything that a poet or a painter could dream of, nature has created in that place. An immense panorama, infinite detail, inexhaustible variety, confused forms, distinct outlines, vague distances, everything is there and Art can add nothing. The mind is not always content to taste and understand God's work and if it thinks of itself, it is to feel its helplessness in creating any expression of this immensity of life, that enthrals and intoxicates us. I advise anyone who is consumed by artistic vanity to look well at these scenes and to look often. It seems to me that they would feel a certain respect for the divine art of the Divinity, that directs the eternal creation of things and which I imagine from their behaviour is lacking in them.

As for myself, I have never been more aware of the emptiness of words than during the hours I spent in contemplation at the Charterhouse. Many religious yearnings came to me but I couldn't think of any other way of expressing them, but like this:

'Dear God, blessed art thou for giving me good eyes!'

For the rest, I believe that if occasional joy in these beautiful spectacles is refreshing and healthy, their continual possession is dangerous. One grows used to living under the power of the senses and the rule that governs the abuse of the senses is nervous irritation. This is how the general indifference of the monks to the poetry of their monasteries can be explained, and the peasants and shepherds to the beauty of their mountains.

We didn't have time to get bored with all this, for the mist descended almost every evening at sunset and hastened the rush of days, already too short, that we would have in that environment. Until midday, we were enveloped by the shadow of the great mountain on our left and by three o'clock we had fallen back into the shadow of the one on our right. But what beautiful effects of light we could study as the slanting rays poured through the cracks in the rocks, or shone between the mountain tops, tracing the middle distance with crests of gold and purple. Sometimes the heads of our cypresses, like black obelisks in the background of the picture, were bathed in this liquid embrace; the bunches of dates on our palm trees resembled clusters of rubies, and a long shadow, cutting the valley diagonally, divided it into two zones, one flooded in summer light, the other appearing as blue and cold as a winter landscape.

The Charterhouse in Valldemossa, following the Carthusian rule and containing exactly thirteen monks, including the Abbot, escaped the decree that in 1836 ordered the destruction of all monasteries of less than twelve occupants; but like all the others, the community of monks was dissolved and the monastery suppressed, that is to say, considered the domain of the State. The State of Mallorca, not knowing what to do with these huge buildings, came to the decision that, while they waited for them to fall down, they would lease the cells to anyone who wanted to live there. Although the price of the leases was extremely moderate, the villagers of Valldemossa did not want to profit from it, perhaps because of their extreme devotion and regard for the monks, perhaps also from superstitious fear. This didn't prevent them from coming to dance on the nights of carnival, as I will explain later, but it made them look very badly at our irreverent presence within its time honoured walls.

Although the Charterhouse is mainly occupied during the summer heat by the townspeople of Palma, who come to find fresher air at these altitudes and within these deep vaults than on the plain or in the city. At the beginning of winter, the cold chases them away, and while we were living there the only inhabitants of the Charterhouse other than myself and my family, were the chemist, the sacristan and Maria Antonia.

Maria Antonia was a kind of housekeeper who had come from Spain to escape, I believe, from poverty and who had rented a cell in order to exploit the temporary visitors to the Charterhouse. Her cell was situated next to ours and served as our kitchen, while the lady was supposed to serve as our housekeeper. She had been a pretty woman, slim and neat in appearance, gentle, and considered herself well born, having charming manners, a harmonious sounding voice, a wheedling manner and exerting a very particular form of hospitality. She was in the habit of offering her services to new arrivals and refusing any kind of compensation for her efforts, with an air of outrage, almost covering her face. She did this, she would say, for the love of God, to be of help, and for the sole reason of making friends with her neighbours. She owned, in the way of furniture, a camp bed, a stove, a brazier, two straw backed chairs, a crucifix and a few earthenware plates. She put all these at your disposal (very generously) and you could leave your servant and your cooking pot in her home.

But as soon as she took possession of all your belongings, she would reserve for herself the best of your clothes and your dinner. I have never seen a pious mouth more greedy, nor fingers more agile at stealing from the bottom of a boiling pot, without getting burnt, nor a throat more elastic at swallowing the sugar or the coffee stolen from her beloved hosts, while continuing to hum a song or a dance tune. It would have been a curious and amusing sight, if one could have been completely disinterested in the situation, to see the good Antonia, with Catalina, the great witch of Valldemossa, who served as our chambermaid, and the 'niña', a scruffy little monster who acted as our groom, all fighting over our dinner.

It was at the hour of the Angelus and the three cats did not forget to recite it; the two older women in duet, their hands lowered into all the plates and the little one responding with 'amen', while pilfering, with unprecedented skill, a cutlet or a candied fruit. It made a good picture and it was well worth the effort to pretend to notice nothing, but as the rain frequently cut off our communications with Palma, and food became scarce, the 'help' from Maria Antonia and her gang became less amusing and we were forced to take it in turns, the children and I, to stand guard over our provisions. I remember, hiding, almost under my pillow, some baskets of biscuits that were needed for breakfast the next day, and standing, like a vulture, over certain plates of fish, to rid our cooking stove of those

plundering little birds that would have left us nothing but the bones.

The sacristan was a hefty fellow, who had perhaps served mass to the Carthusians in his youth and ever since had been the custodian of the monastery keys. He had a scandulous history to account for; he had been caught and convicted of seducing and bringing to a bad end a young lady who had spent a few months at the Charterhouse with her parents, and he claimed as an excuse that he had been employed by the State to protect only the virgins in the holy paintings.

He was not the most handsome man in the world but he saw himself as a dandy. Instead of the attractive, partly Arabic dress, worn by the people of his class, he wore European trousers and braces, which certainly caught the eye of the local girls. His sister was the most beautiful Mallorquin girl that I have seen. He didn't live in the monastery, they were rich and proud and had a house in the village, but they made the rounds each day and visited Maria Antonia, who invited them to eat our dinner when she wasn't feeling hungry.

The apothecary was a Carthusian monk who would close himself in his cell, wear his faded white habit and recite his prayers alone in a grand manner. When one rang at his door to ask him for marsh-mallow or couch-grass, (the only medicines he possessed), he would throw his cowl hastily under the bed and appear in black breeches, stockings and a little waist-coat, just like the costums of the Operatic characters that Moliere employes to dance ballet during the intervals. He was a very suspicious old man, he never complained about anything, and perhaps he prayed for the triumph of Don Carlos and the return of the Holy Inquisition, but without wishing to hurt any-one. He sold us his couch-grass at the price of gold, and consoled himself with these little profits for having been released from the vow of poverty. His cell was a long way from ours, at the entrance to the monastery, in a kind of recess, where the door was hidden behind a castor oil bush and other healthy medicinal plants. Hidden there like an old hare who is afraid of putting the dogs on his trail, he never went out, and if we had not called on him several times to ask him for his juleps, we would never have been sure if there was still a monk in the Charterhouse.

This Charterhouse has nothing of architectural beauty, but it is a collection of large, well construct-ed buildings, with such a large, enclosed area and with such a great mass of carved stone, that it could have housed an army corps, and yet that huge edifi-ce had been built for twelve people. In the new cloi-ster alone, (for the monastery consists of three Charterhouses, connected to one another at different periods), there are twelve cells, each of three large rooms, facing one side of the cloister. On the two sides are twelve chapels. Each monk had his own in which he closed himself to pray alone. All the chapels were variously decorated, covered with gilt and paintings of very bad taste, with statues of saints in coloured wood, so horrible that I would not like to meet them, I have to confess, out of their niches at night. The paving in these oratories is made from grazed earthenware tiles and arranged in many, very effective, mosaic designs. The Arabic style is still in evidence here and is the only tradition in good taste that has come down through the centuries in Mallorca. Finally, every one of these chapels is equipped with a fountain where, from a shell of local marble, each monk had to wash his oratory every day. A freshness prevails in these dark vaulted rooms, paved with enamel tiles, which must have given the long hours of prayer during the burning heat of the Dog days a sort of sensual pleasure.

The fourth side of the new cloister, at the centre of which stands a small courtyard planted with symmetrical box trees which have not yet completely lost the triangular shapes cut by the monk's shears, lies parallel to an attractive church, the freshness and cleanliness of which contrasts with the neglect and emptiness of the monastery. We hoped to find an organ there; we had forgotten that the Carthusian rule forbids every type of musical instrument as vain luxury and sensual pleasure. The church consists of a single nave, paved with beautiful earthenware tiles, delicately painted with bouquets of flowers arranged like a carpet. The wooden panelling, the confessionals and the doors are very simple; but their perfect lines and the clean workmanship soberly and delicately decorated, attest to handiwork that is no longer found in French carpentry. Unfortunately this careful workmanship has also been lost in Mallorca. There are only two carpenters in the whole of the island, according to M. Tastu, who have continued to treat their work as an art. The carpenter we employed at the Charterhouse was certainly an artist, but only in music and painting. Arriving at our cell one day to put up some white wood shelves, he looked at all our painting equipment with the same naive and impertinent curiosity that I have noticed before among the Slavonic Greeks. The sketches my son had made from Goya's drawings of monks at an orgy that decorated our room, shocked him a bit; but seeing an engraving of Rubens' Descent from the Cross, he stood for a long time absorbed in a strange contemplation. We asked him what he thought of it. 'There is nothing in the whole of Mallorca,' he told us in his dialect. 'so beautiful and so natural.'

The word 'natural' coming from the lips of a peasant with the hair and manners of a savage, surprised us a lot. The sound of the piano and the playing of an artist threw him into a kind of ecstasy. He would

174

leave his work and come to stand behind the pianist's chair, his mouth half open and his eyes standing out from his head. These higher instincts did not prevent him from being a thief, as all Mallorquin peasants are with foreigners; without any kind of scruple, however religiously loyal they are said to be in their dealings with each other. He asked a fabulous price for his work, and eagerly put his hands on every little object, made in France, that we had brought for our own use. I had a lot of difficulty saving my toilet requisites from his large pockets. What tempted him most was a cut glass tumbler, or perhaps it was the toothbrush inside it, while he certainly did not understand its use. That man had an Italian yearning for art and the thieving instincts of a Malay or a Kaffir.

This digression has not made me forget to mention the one work of art we did find at the Charterhouse. It was a statue of Saint Bruno in painted wood standing in the church. The outline and the colour of it was remarkable; the carefully studied hands evoked a vivid impression of piety and anguish; the head had a truly sublime expression of faith and pain. And yet, it was the work of an ignorant man; for the statue in front of it, carved by the same hand, was pitiful in every respect; he must have had a flash of inspiration when he created Saint Bruno, a breath of religious fervour perhaps, that lifted him above himself. I doubt if the fanatical saint of Grenoble has ever been understood or portrayed with such deep and burning emotion. It was the personification of Christian asceticism. But in Mallorca this symbol of a bygone philosophy is left to stand in solitude.

The old cloister which had to be crossed to reach the new one, was connected to it by a very simple detour which, thanks to my poor sense of direction, I could never find without first losing myself in the third cloister.

The third building, which I ought to call the first because it is the oldest, is also the smallest. It has a charming appearance. The courtyard, which is enclosed by its crumbling walls, is the ancient cemetery of the monks. No inscriptions mark these graves, which the monk had to dig during his lifetime and where nothing could dispute his memory once it was annihilated by death. The tombs are only visible as swellings in the turf. M. Laurens has recorded the features of this cloister in an attractive drawing where I rediscovered, with incredible delight, the little well with the steep roof, the windows crossed in stone where all the weeds wandering over the ruins hung in festoons and the tall cypresses that stand at night like black ghosts around the white wood cross. I was annoyed that he had not seen the moon rising behind the beautiful mountain of amber coloured sandstone that dominates the cloister and that he did not put the old laurel bush in the foreground, with its enormous trunk and dried branches, which perhaps no longer existed by the time he visited the Charter-house. But I did find in his drawing as well as in his text an honorable mention of the lovely dwarf palm tree (Chamoerops) that I defended against the naturistic enthusiam of my children and which is perhaps the most vigorous example of its species in Europe.

The old, fifteenth century chapels are arranged a-round this small cloister. They are hermatically sealed and the sacristan will not open them to anyone, which really spiced our curiosity. By looking through the cracks during our walks, we believed we could see a beautiful jumble of furnishings and ancient wooden sculptures. One could probably find a lot of hidden treasures in those mysterious garrets from which nobody in Mallorca will even bother to remo-ve the dust.

The second cloister has twelve cells and twelve chapels like the others. Its decaying arcades have a lot of character. There is nothing left of them and when we crossed there at night in bad weather, we would put ourselves in God's hand, for a storm never broke over the Charterhouse without a piece of wall or a fragment of an old archway falling down. I have never heard the wind howling as mournfully or shrie-king as desperately as in those broken and echoing galleries. The sound of rushing water, the headlong race of the clouds, the great, monotonous roar of the sea was interrupted by the whistling of the storm and the cries of the sea birds that flew past, all frightened and confused in the gusts; then the great mists that fell suddenly like a shroud and penetrated the cloister through the broken arches, made us invisible and made the little lamp that we were carrying to guide us, appear like a playful spirit wandering under the galleries, and a thousand other details of this monastic life that crowd all at once into my memory: all the things that made our stay at the Charterhouse the most romantic on earth.

I didn't mind seeing in reality, for once, what I had only seen in dreams, or in fashionable ballads or during the nun's act in 'Robert le Diable' at the Opera. Even fantastic apparitions were not missing, which I will tell you about in a minute: and with regard to all this romanticism appearing before me, I couldn't help making a few comments on romanticism in general.

As well as the mass of buildings I have just described, the part reserved for the prior must be added, which we were not allowed to visit, nor many other mysterious corners; the cells of the lay brothers, the little church adjoining the ancient Charterhouse and several other buildings destined for important people who came there on retreat or to perform devotions of penance. Several little courtyards surrounded by stables for the animals of the community, lodgings for the numerous visitors; in fact, a whole 'phalanstery', as one would say nowadays, under the protection of the Virgin and Saint Bruno.

When the weather was so bad that it prevented us from climbing the mountain, we took our walk under cover inside the monastery, and we needed several hours to explore the enormous manor. I don't know what attracted my curiosity and urged me to find the believed that I could hear the sound of sandals on the paving stones and the murmur of prayers under the chapel vaults. Prayers in Latin printed and stuck to the walls of our cells could still be read, even in secret places where I would never have imagined anyone would say the 'oremus'.

One day when we went to explore the upper galleries, we found a pretty platform in front of us, from which we could look down into a large and beautiful chapel, so well arranged and furnished that one would have said it had been abandoned the day before. The Abbot's armchair was still in place and the order of the weekly religious services, attached to a frame of black wood, hung from the ceiling in the midst of the chapter stalls. Each stall had a small picture of a saint attached to the back, which was probably the patron saint of each monk. The smell of incense that has impregnated the walls for so long had not yet completely disappeared. The altars were adorned with dried flowers and half burned torches still stood in their holders. The order and conservation of these objects contrasted with the ruins outside, the height of the brambles that covered the windows and the cries of the little rascals who played at quoits among the cloisters with pieces of mosaic.

As for my children, their sense of wonder became even more lively during these enjoyable and exciting expeditions. My daughter certainly expected to find some fairy palace, filled with marvals, in the attics of the Charterhouse, and my son hoped to discover the traces of some dreadful and bizarre drama hidden under the rubble. I was often horrified to see them climbing like cats over warped planks and shaky terraces. And when they got a few steps ahead of me and disappeared around the turn of a spiral staircase, I thought that I had lost them and I doubled my steps, with a kind of terror in which superstition perhaps counted for something.

For one cannot deny that these sinister places, dedicated to an even more sinister cult, stir the imagination a little, and I will defy the most calm and indifferent brain to remain there for very long in a state of perfect sanity. These fanciful little fears, if I may call them that, are not without their appeal; and yet they are real enough for it to be necessary to combat them in oneself. I swear that I never crossed the cloister at night without feeling a certain mixture of anxiety and pleasure, which I didn't want to show in front of my children, in the belief that I would communicate it to them. Yet they didn't appear to be concerned and they ran freely in the moonlight under the broken arches that really seemed to invite the sabbat dances. I led them through the cemetery several times around midnight.

However I no longer allowed them to go out alone at night, after we had met an old man who sometimes walked in the darkness. He was an old servant or tenant of the community, whose mind was often confused by a mixture of wine and devotion. When he was drunk, he would come and wander around the cloisters, knocking on the doors of the empty cells with a large pilgrim's staff, from which hung a long rosary , and calling the monks with his drunken ranting and praying in a mournful voice outside the chapels. As he noticed a bit of light escaping from our cell, it was there, most of all, that he came to prowl with his threats and his terrible oaths. He entered Maria Antonia's cell, who was very afraid of him, and gave her long sermons, interrupted with cynical oaths. He installed himself beside her brazier until the sacristan came to extract him with compliments and cunning; for the sacristan was not very brave and feared that he would make himself an enemy. Then the man would come and knock on our door at unreasonbale hours; and when he got tired of calling on Father Nicolas in vain, which was his only idea, he would fall at the feet of the Madonna, whose niche was only a few paces from our door and go to sleep there, his knife open in one hand and his string of beads in the other.

His uproar didn't worry us very much, because he was not a man who would throw himself at anyone unexpectedly. As he announced his presence from a distance with his interrupted shouting and the sound of his stick on the paving, one had time to beat a retreat before this wild animal, and the double door of solid oak to our cell could have held back an equally formidable siege; but this obstinate assault, while we had a weakened invalid who needed some hours of rest, was not always comical. It had to be overcome however with 'mucha calma', for we would certainly not have received any protection from the local police; we never went to mass and our enemy was a saintly man who never missed a single service.

One night, we had an alarm and an apparition of another kind, that I will never forget. First of all, there was an unexplained noise that I can only compare with the sound of thousands of sacks of nuts rolling continually over the floor. We hurried out into the cloister to see what it could be. The cloister was deserted and dark as usual; but the noise still approached without interruption and soon a faint light lit up the vast depth of the vaults. Bit by bit they were illuminated by the flames of several torches, and we saw appearing, in the red smoke that surrounded them, a crowd of horrible beings abomin-able to God and to man. It was no less than Lucifer in person, attended by his entire court, a devil master, completely black, with horns and a face the colour of blood; and all around him a host of devils with bird's heads and horses' tails, and tincels of every colour, and she-devils and shepherdesses dressed in pink and white, who appeared to have been carried off by these evil gnomes. After the confession that I have just made, I admit that for one or two minutes and even a little while after I had realised what it was, it required a certain effort of will for me to hold up my lamp to the level of that ugly masquerade, at that time of night when the place and the torchlight created a truly supernatural effect.

They were the people of the village, wealthy farmers and small tradesmen, celebrating the festival of Mardi Gras and coming to begin their rustic dance in Maria Antonia's cell. The strange noise that accompanied them was the sound of castanets, which several boys wearing dirty, hideous masks were all playing at once, and not in a controlled and regular rhythm like in Spain but with a continual rumble like that of a drum beating in the fields.

This noise, which accompanies their dances, is so dry and so harsh that it needs courage to stand it for a quarter of an hour. During their festive processions, they would suddenly interrupt it to sing a 'coplita' in unison, on one phrase of music that kept repeating itself and never seemed to end; then the castanets would begin to rumble again for three or four minutes. Nothing could be more savage than this method of playing, that shatters the eardrums with the clapping of wood. The musical phrase, which is nothing on its own, takes on a greater significance when uttered like this over long periods of time, and by these voices which also have a very personal character. They are veiled in their loudest outbursts and they drag when most animated...

I imagine that the Arabs sang like this, and M. Tastu, who did some research in this respect, was convinced that the principal Mallorquin rhythms and their favourite embellishments, that their style in fact, is of an Arabic type and tradition.

When we were sailing from Barcelona to Palma, on a warm, dark night, illuminated by an extraordinary phosphorescence in the ship's wake, everyone on board was asleep except for the helmsman who, in order to resist doing likewise, sang all night long, but in such a soft and careful voice that one would think he was afraid of waking the men of the night watch or that he was half asleep himself. We never tired of listening to him, for his singing was so strange. He followed a rhythm and modulations that were beyond all our experience, and seemed to let his voice wander at random, like the smoke from the funnel that was carried and balanced on the breeze. It was more like a dream than a song, where thought hardly took part, but which followed the rolling of the ship, the faint sound of the swell and which resembled a vague improvisation, yet confined within its soft, monotonous form.

This thoughtful voice had great charm.

When all the devils reached us, they surrounded us with friendly politeness, for the Mallorquins are never sullen or hostile, generally, in their manner. The King Beelzebub deigned to say a word to me in Spanish and told me that he was a lawyer. Then he tried to give me a good impression of himself by speaking to me in French and, wanting to ask me if I liked the Charterhouse, he translated the Spanish word 'cartuxa' into the French word 'cartouche' which could not help causing a slight misunderstanding. But a Mallorquin devil does not have to speak every language.

Their dances were no more lively than their songs. We followed them into Maria Antonia's cell, which was decorated with little paper lanterns hanging across the room from garlands of ivy. An orchestra, composed of one large and one small guitar, a kind of treble violin and three or four pairs of castanets, began to play the native 'jotas' and fandangos, which resembled those of Spain but with a more unusual rhythm and an even more daring arrangement.

This festival was given in honour of Raphael Torres, a wealthy local tenant, who had married quite a pretty girl a few days earlier. The new husband was the only man condemned to dance almost all evening in front of each woman in turn, as they invited him one by one. During the duet, the whole gathering sat silently and solemnly on the ground, squatting in an Oriental or African manner. Even the mayor himself, in his monk's cape and with his large, black staff capped with silver.

The Mallorquin 'boleros' have an ancestral gravity and none of the rough grace that one admires in Andalucia. Men and women hold their arms out rigidly, their fingers continuously and rapidly roll their castanets. The handsome Raphael danced to clear his conscience. When he had done his duty, he went to sit, crouched like a dog with the others and the local roques took their turns to come and shine. One young boy, as slim as a wasp, won the admiration of all with the rigidity of his movements and his leaps on the spot, like electric springs, without letting his face show the slightest sign of joy. A hefty labourer, very stylish and conceited, tried to lift his leg and extend his arms in the Spanish manner; he was jeered at, which he well deserved, but it was the most laughable caricature to be seen. We would have been captivated by these rustic dances for a long time, but for the smell of rancid oil and garlic that these men and women exhaled and which really stuck in one's throat.

The carnival disguises were not as interesting to us as the native dress; which is very elegant and graceful. The women wear a kind of white lace or muslin wimple, called a 'rebozillo', made from two pieces superimposed; one that is attached to the back of the head, passing underneath the chin, like a nun's coif, and which is called 'rebozillo en amount' and another which hangs like a cape over the shoulders and is called 'rebozillo en volant.' The hair, neatly parted into smooth bands on the forehead, is joined at the back in a long plait that hangs below the 'rebozillo', falls down the back and is lifted to one side and tucked into the belt. Unadorned during the week, the unplaited hair is left to flow down the back in 'estoffade'. The bodice, of wool or black silk, low cut with short sleeves, is decorated around the elbow and along the back seams with metal buttons and silver chains very tastefully attached to the buttons with great style and richness. They are slim with a small waist, tiny feet and elegantly shod on feast days. A simple village girl wears stockings by day, satin shoes, a gold chain around her neck and several bands of silver chains around the waist and hanging from her belt. I have seen many with very well made bodies, few that were pretty; their features were regular, like the Andalucian girls, but with more innocent and gentle expressions. In the Soller district, which I never visited, they had a reputation for their beauty.

The men that I saw were not handsome but they appeared to be at first sight because of the flattering costume they wore. It consisted on Sundays of a waistcoat (guarde pit) of multi-coloured silk material, cut in a heart-shape and open over the chest, like the black jacket (sayo), short and fitting at the waist like the woman's bodice. A splendidly white shirt, attached at the neck and at the wrists with embroidered bands, leaves the neck bare and the chest covered in beautiful linen, which always adds brilliance to the costume. Their waists are tied by a coloured sash over large, billowing trousers like a Turks, in wide stripes of cotton or silk material, which is made locally on the island. With this, they have white, black or fawn linen stockings and shoes of undressed and unstained calf skin. A wide brimmed hat of 'moxine' or wild cat fur, with laces and black tassels of gold and silk thread, detracts from the Oriental character of this addition. Indoors, they wrap a scarf or an Indian handkerchief around their heads, like a turban, which suits them far better. In winter, they often wear a black woollen skull cap that covers the top of the head, for they shave their crowns like priests, either as a measure of cleanliness, and God knows it doesn't do them much good, or a a sign of devotion. Their thick mane, rough and frizzy, flows therefore around their necks (as far as hair can be said to flow) line cut with scissors across the forehead completes this hairstyle, shaped exactly in the style of the Middle Ages and which gives every face a forceful look.

In the fields, their clothes are more simple and even more picturesque. They leave their legs bare or covered in yellow leather gaiters up to the knee, according to the season. When it is hot, they only wear a shirt and pantaloons. In winter, they cover themselves with a grey cape, that looks like a monk's cloak or with a large African goat's skin, with the hair outwards. When they walk in a group with these fawn coloured skins, which have a black line down the back and which hang from their heads to their feet, one could easily take them to be a herd of goats walking on their hind legs. When they go to the fields or return home, one of them almost always walks in front, playing a guitar or a flute, and the others follow in silence, treading in his footsteps and hanging their heads with an air of complete innocence and stupidly. They do not lack shrewdness, however foolish they seem from their appearance.

They are usually tall, and their dress makes them appear very slim, and that makes them seem taller still. Their necks, which are always exposed to the air, are strong and handsome; their chests, freed from tight waistcoats and braces, are open and well developed; but almost all of them have bandy legs.

We thought that the old and more mature men had, if not handsome features, at least serious and very noble traits. They all resembled monks, as they are depicted poetically. The younger generation seemed common to us and of a jovial type, that breaks at once the connection. Is it only twenty years since the monks stopped interfering in domestic intimacy?

This is nothing but a facetious traveller's joke.

CHAPTER TWO

I said earlier that I searched to discover the secret of monastic life in a place where its traces were still so recent. I don't mean by this that I wanted to unearth any mysterious facts relating to this particular Charterhouse, but I did ask those abandoned walls to reveal the intimate thoughts of those silent monks to me, which for centuries had separated them from human life. I would have liked to follow the frayed or broken thread of Christian faith through the souls that were thrown there by each generation, like a sacrifice to a jealous God, who needed human victims as much as the pagan gods did. In the end I would have liked to bring to life a fifteenth century monk and one from the nineteenth century, to compare two Catholics separated in their faith, without knowing it, by an abyss and to ask each of them what they thought of the other..

It seemed to me that the life of the first would be

191

quite easy to reconstruct accurately in my mind. I saw that mediaeval Christian all of a piece, devoted, sincere, brokenhearted by the sight of war, disorder and the suffering of his contemporaries, escaping that evil void and searching in ascetic meditation to free and detach himself as far as possible from a life where the idea of the perfectibility of the masses as a concept was not yet available to the individual. But the Carthusian monk of the nineteenth century, closing his eyes to the progress of humanity, that had become possible and obvious, indifferent to the lives of other men, no longer understood either religion or the Pope, or the church, or society, or himself, and no longer seeing anything more in his Charterhouse than a spacious, comfortable and safe residence or anything more in his vocation than a secure existence, an opportunity to indulge his instincts with impunity and a means of acquiring, without personal merit, the admiration and consideration of devout Christians, peasants and women, that I cannot show so easily. I cannot appreciate exactly how great his remorse, blindness, hypocrisy or sincerity must have been. It would have been impossible for that man to have had true faith in the Roman Church, unless he was completely devoid of intelligence. It would have been equally impossible for him to be a pronounced atheist, or his entire life would be an odious lie, and I cannot believe in a totally stupid man or one who is completely vile. It is the image of his internal battles, of his alternating revolt and submission, of his philosophical doubts and his superstitious terror that I saw before my eyes like an inferno: and the more I identified with that last Carthusian monk, who lived in my cell before me, the more I felt the weight of the anxieties and agitations I attributed to him in my spirited imagination.

It was enough to cast one's eyes over the ancient cloisters and then over the modern Charterhouse to observe the changes in the need for comfort, hygiene and even elegance that had slipped into the lives of these reclusive monks, but also to notice the slackening in monastic habits and in the spirit of mortification and penitence. For whereas all the old cells were dark, narrow and badly fitted, the new ones were bright, airy and well constructed. I will describe the cell that we inhabited to give an idea of the severity of the Carthusian rule, even when it was evaded and softened as much as possible.

It consisted of three spacious rooms, with elegantly vaulted ceilings and ventilated with openwork rosettes, all of distinct and very attractive designs. These three rooms were separated from the cloister by a dark turning and closed with a strong oak door. The walls were three feet thick. The middle room was intended for reading, prayer and meditation, all the furniture it contained was a large chair and prayer stool, with a headboard, six to eight feet in height, firmly fixed to the wall. The room on the right of this one was the monk's bedroom; at the end was a very low alcove, covered with stone slabs like a tomb. The room on the left was the workroom, dining room and store room of the recluse. At the far end stood a cupboard with a wooden panel, that opened like a hatch onto the cloister, through which he was passed his food. His kitchen consisted of two small stoves, situated out of doors but no longer in the open air, as the rule strictly demanded. A covered arch over the garden protected the monk's culinary operations from the rain and allowed him to devote a little more time to this activity than the founder would have liked. What's more, a fireplace introduced into the third room indicated even more laxity, even though the knowledge of the architect was not sufficient to make it work.

The entire apartment had a long, dark, narrow passage at the back, at the level of the rosettes, in order to ventilate the cell, and a loft above it for drying corn, onions, beans and other frugal winter provisions. To the south, the three rooms opened onto a garden plot, extending exactly the same length as the whole cell, that was divided by ten foot walls from the neighbouring gardens and that rested on a solidly built stone terrace, overlooking a little orange grove that occupied the mountain terrace. The terrace belowthat was filled with a beautiful grape bower, the third with almond and palm trees, and so on down to the bottom of the valley, which, as I have said, was one enormous garden.

parce que je ne connais pas
de banquier à Palma. —
Puisque vous avez voulu, chère[?]
prendre la corvée d'être mon
éditeur — il faut que je vous avert[?]
qu'il y a encore des manuscrits
à vos ordres. — la ballade
(qui est encore dans les engagem[ents]
Probst pour l'Allemagne) —
cette ballade — j'en veux mille fr.
pour la France et l'Angleterre.
2do Deux polonaises (dont vous
connaissez une en la) — j'en veux
mille cinq cents fr. pour tous les
pays du globe — 3° Un 3me
Scherzo — même prix que les
Polonaises pour toute l'Europe.
Cela vous arrivera sur le doigt[?]

si vous le voulez d[?]
jusqu'à l'arrivé de
vous dirai plus qu[?]
écrire. — Je n'ai ...
nouvelles qu'indirec[tes]
Fontana qui va ...
aller mieux — ...
... d'une organisati[on]
J'attends 3 mois une
Varsovie. — Et les
Mme Pleyel? — M...
Dites leur toutes les
souhaits pour l'ann[ée]
une lettre de Nous —...
toute petite — et ...
comme toujours ...

Sendmuva[?] moi mon autogr[aphe]
Valldemosa près Palma

15

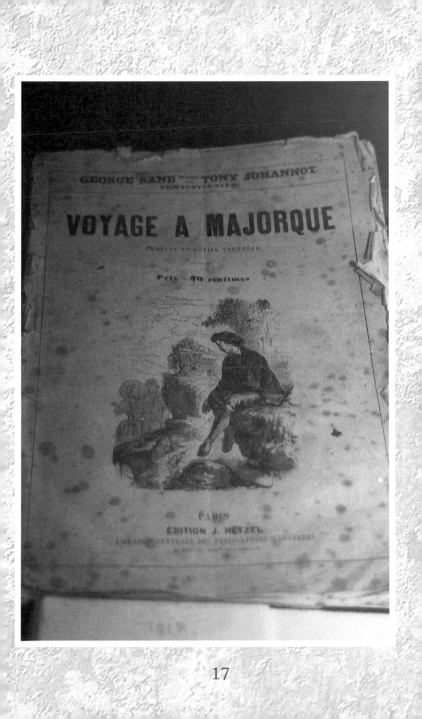

GEORGE SAND ... TONY JOHANNOT

VOYAGE A MAJORQUE

PRÉFACE ET NOTICE NOUVELLE

Prix : 40 centimes

PARIS
ÉDITION J. HETZEL
LIBRAIRIE CENTRALE DES PUBLICATIONS ILLUSTRÉES

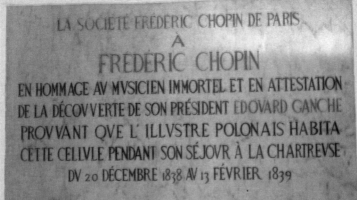

The garden of every cell had a carved stone cistern along the right side of it, three or four feet long and of an equal depth, that collected mountain water from the canals along the edge of the terrace into the four separate channels. I never understood such an abundance of water to quench the thirst of just one man, nor such a luxurious method of irrigation for a garden of twenty feet in diameter. If one hadn't known the monks' particular dislike for bathing and the abstemious habits of the Mallorquin in this respect, one would have imagined that the good Carthusians spent their lives washing themselves, like Indian priests.

As for this garden, planted with pomegranate, lemon and orange trees, surrounded by raised brick paths and sheltered, like the cistern with sweet scented arbours, it resembled a lovely room of flowers and greenery, where the monk could walk with dry feet on wet days and refresh his lawns with a sheet of running water on hot days, smell the fragrance of oranges from the edge of a beautiful terrace, where their bushy shapes rose like domes resplendent with fruit and flowers before his eyes, and gaze in complete tranquillity at a landscape, that was both graceful and austere, melancholy and magnificent, as I have already mentioned; and even cultivate rare and precious flowers to delight his eye, gather the most delicious fruit to quench his thirst, listen to the gentle sound of the sea, contemplate the splendour of summer nights beneath the most beautiful sky and adore Eternity in the most beautiful temple that was ever opened to man in the heart of nature.

This was how the indescribable delights of the Carthusians appeared to me at first, this was what I promised myself when I moved into one of their cells, which seemed to have been arranged purely to satisfy the wonderful whims of the imagination or the dreams of a chosen band of poets and artists.

But when one is faced with the existence of a man without intelligence and therefore without dreams and imagination, even perhaps without faith, that is to say, without enthusiasm and contemplation, buried in this cell with its massive, deaf and dumb walls, subdued by the brutal restrictions of the order and forced to observe the word, without understanding its meaning, condemned to the horror of loneliness, reduced to seeing the heights of the mountains and the human species creeping along the valley floor, only from a distance, to remain eternally a stranger to the other captive souls, sworn to the same silence, closed in the same tomb, forever neighbours and forever separated, even in prayer; finally, when one feels oneself, a free and thoughtful being, led out of sympathy into certain fears and failings, all this becomes sad and depressing like a life of emptiness, error and impotence.

Then one can understand the incomparable boredom of this monk, on whom nature has wasted her most beautiful views and who cannot enjoy them because he has no-one else with whom to share his enjoyment; the brutal sadness of this penitent who can feel nothing but hot and cold, like a plant; and the mortal chill of this Christian, for whom nothing can animate or revitalise the spirit of ascetisism. Condemned to eat alone, work alone, suffer and pray alone, he could only have had one desire to escape this dreadful confinement; and I was told that the last Carthusians showed so little restraint, that some of them were absent for weeks and months on end, without the Prior being able to get them to return to the Order.

I'm afraid that I have made a long and detailed description of our Charterhouse, without giving any idea of what delighted us about it at the beginning and why its poetry was lost to us when we examined it more closely. I gave in, as I always do, to the influence of my memories and now that I have tried to convey my impressions, I wonder why I could not have said in twenty lines what I have said in twenty pages. Knowing that a carefree peace of mind, and all that it involves, appears delightful to a tired soul, but upon reflection its charm vanishes. Only a genius can draw a complete and vivid picture in one stroke of the brush. When M. Lamennais visited the Camaldulians in Tivoli, he was seized by the same emotion and expressed it in a masterly way:

"We arrived at their house,' he said, 'at the hour of communal prayer. They all appeared to be quite old and taller than average. Lining both sides of the nave, they remained kneeling after the service, without moving, deep in meditation. One would have said that they no longer belonged to this earth; their shaven heads bowed under other thoughts and other cares; no outward movement, no external sign of life, wrapped in their long white cloaks, they resembled those statues that pray on old tombs.'

'We could understand very well the kind of attraction this solitary existence holds for certain world-weary and disillusioned souls. Who has not aspired to something similar? Who has not, more than once, turned his eyes towards the desert and dreamed of peace in a corner of the forest, or in a mountain grotto, close to an unknown spring where the birds of the heavens come to drink?'

'However, none of this is the true destination of man; he is born for action; he has a task to accomplish. What does it matter if it is difficult? Is it not only offered for love?' ('Affaires de Rome.')

The short piece, so full of images, inspiration, ideas and profound thoughts, thrown almost by chance in the middle of M. Lamennais' account of his experiences at the Holy See, has always impressed me, and I am certain that one day it will provide some great painter with the subject for a painting. On one side, the Camaldulites at prayer, obscure, placid monks, forever useless, forever powerless, ghosts bent in prayer, the last examples of a cult about to return to the darkness of the past, kneeling on the stone of a tomb as cold and mournful as they are; on the other side, the man of the future, the last priest, enlivened by the last spark of genius of the Church, meditating on the fate of those monks, observing them like an artist, judging them philosophically. Here, the Levites of death motionless under their shrouds; there, the apostle of life, the tireless traveller in the infinite fields of thought, already bidding a last, sympathetic farewell to the poetry of the cloister; and shaking the dust of the Papal city from his feet, to rush towards the holy road of moral freedom.

I have collected no other historical facts about my Charterhouse except for the sermon preached by Saint Vincent Ferrier in Valldemossa, and once again I owe the exact account to M. Tastu. This sermon was an important event in Majorca in 1413, and it is interesting to learn how eagerly they wanted a missionary at that time, and how solemnly he was received.

'The Mallorquins had met in 1409 in a large assembly and decided to write to Master Vincent Ferrier, or Ferrier, to ask him to come and preach in Majorca. It was Don Luis de Prades, Bishop of Majorca, camerlingo of Pope Benedict XIII, (the Anti-pope Peter de

Luna), who wrote a letter in 1412 to the aldermen of Valencia to beg for apostolic aid from Master Vincent and who met him the following year in Barcelona and travelled with him to Palma. On the day after his arrival the saintly missionary began his sermons and ordered nocturnal processions. The island was suffering from a very severe drought; but during Master Vincent's third sermon the rain fell. These details were sent to King Ferdinand by the Royal Prosecutor, Don Pedro de Casaldaguila:

'Most High, Most Excellent Prince and Victorious Lord,

I have the honour of anouncing to you that Master Vincent has arrived in this city on the first day of September, and that he was solemnly received. On Saturday morning, he began to preach before an immense crowd, who listened to him with such devotion that every night there are processions in which one sees men, women and children scourging themselves. As no rain has fallen for a long time, the Lord God, moved by the prayers of the children and the people, desired that this realm, that was dying from drought, should see the rain fall during the third sermon, abundantly all over the island, which caused great rejoicing among the inhabitants.

May our Lord God aid you for many years, Most Victorious Lord, and exalt your royal crown.'
Majorca, 11th September 1413.

200

The crowd that wanted to hear the missionary Saint grew so large that it couldn't fit into the vast church of the Convent of the Dominicans and they were obliged to make the immense garden of the monastery available to them, by erecting stands and pulling down walls.

Vincent Ferrier preached in Palma until 3rd October and then left to tour the island. His first stop was at Valldemossa, in the monastery that intended to receive and house him and which he had chosen no doubt because of his brother Boniface, who was General of the Carthusian Order. The prior of Valldemossa had come to fetch him in Palma and to accompany him. In Valldemossa, even more than in Palma, the church was found to be too small to hold the eager crowd.

Here is the Chronicler's report:

'The town of Valldemossa preserves the memory of the time when Saint Vincent Ferrier sowed the divine word there. Within the district of Valldemossa, there is a property called 'Son Gual'. The missionary was taken there, followed by an infinite multitude. The area was large and flat; the hollow trunk of an ancient and enormous olive tree served him as a pulpit. As soon as the Saint spoke from the top of the olive tree, the rain began to fall heavily. The devil, promoter of wind, lightning and thunder, seemed to want to force his listeners to leave and shelter under cover, which is what some of them had already begun to do when Vincent ordered them to keep still and began to pray, and at that moment a cloud spread like a canopy over him and over those who were listening to him, although the men who had continued to work in the adjoining field were forced to leave their work.

'The old trunk still existed a century ago, for our forefathers religiously preserved it. Then the heirs of 'Son Gual' neglected to care for this holy object and its memory was forgotten. But God never wanted the rustic pulpit of Saint Vincent to be lost. The servants of the estate, looking for wood, caught sight of the olive tree with the idea of cutting it up; but their axes instantly broke, and when the news reached the ears of the old people, they cries that it was a miracle and the sacred olive was left in tact. Later on the tree split into thirty-four pieces and although it was within reach of the town, nobody dared to touch it and it was revered as a relic.

'Meanwhile, the saintly preacher went to speak in even the smallest hamlet, healing the bodies and souls of the unfortunate. The only remedy the Saint prescribed was the water of a spring that flowed near Valldemossa. This fountain or spring is still known by the name of 'Sa Bassa Ferrara.'

'Saint Vincent spent six months on the island, until he was recalled by King Ferdinand of Aragon to help him suppress the discord that was disrupting the West. The missionary Saint took leave of the Mallorquins with a sermon in Palma Cathedral, and after blessing his followers, he left to board the ship, accompanied by the jurors, the nobility and a multitude of the people, performing many miracles, according to the tradition that still endures to this day in the Balearic Island.'

This story, which would make Mademoiselle Fanny Elsler smile, leads to a remark by M. Tastu, which is curious for two reasons: in the first place, because it provides a very reasonable explanation for one of Saint Vincent Ferrier's miracles; and in the second place, because it confirms an important fact in the history of language. Here is the note:

'Vincent Ferrier wrote his sermons in Latin, and he pronounced them in the Limousin language. It was considered a miracle that the Saint had the power to be understood by his listeners even when he was speaking a foreign language. Yet nothing could be more natural, if one goes back to the time when Master Vincent flourished. At that time, the Romance languages spoken in the three great regions of the North, the Centre and the South were almost identical. The people, and especially the educated, understood each other very well. Master Vincent was a success in England, Scotland, Ireland, in Paris, Brittany, Italy, Spain and in the Balearic Islands; and it was because in all these countries they understood, even if they couldn't speak, a Romance language, the sister, parent or cousin to the Valencian language that was Vincent Ferrier's mother tongue.'

'After all, wasn't the famous missionary a contemporary of the poet Chaucer, of Jean Froissart, of Christine de Pisan, Boccaccio, Ausias March and so many other famous Europeans?'

The people of the Baleares spoke the ancient Romance language of Limosine, that language which M. Raynouard included, without investigation or distinction, in the language of Provence.

Of all the Romance languages, Mallorquin has undergone fewer variations, being concentrated in the islands where it has been protected from all contact from outside. The language of Languedoc, even today in its diluted and decadent state, the graceful dialect of Montpellier and its surroundings, is the most similar to ancient and modern Mallorquin. This can be explained by the fact that the Kings of Aragon and their courts often stayed in the town of Montpellier. Pedro II, killed at Muret in 1213 while fighting Simon de Montford, married Marie, daughter of a Count of Montpellier, and Jaime I, known as the Conqueror, was born in that town and spent the first years of his childhood there. One of the characteristics that distinguishes the Mallorquin language from other Romance dialects of the Langue d'Oc, are the articles in popular use, and remarkably, these articles are found mainly in the local dialects in certain areas of the Island of Sardinia. Besides the Mallorquin has more articles than the others.

We have to mention in passing that these article, although of ancient usage, were never used in the legal documents that date from the conquest of the Baleares by the Aragonese; that is to say, that in the islands as in the regions of Italy, two languages were used simultaneously; the uneducated '*plebea*', used by the people (which changes very little), and the academic, literary language '*aulica illustra*', which time, civilization or genius perfect and purify. Therefore today, Castilian is the literary language of all of Spain, while each province has kept its dialect for everyday use. In Mallorca, Castilian is hardly used, except in official circumstances; but in the normal life of the people, as well as in the grand nobility, you will hear only Malloquin spoken. If you pass a balcony where a young girl, an 'Alote' (from the Arabic 'aila', 'lella'), is watering her flowers, it will be in her soft, native dialect that you will hear her singing:

Sas atlotes, tots es diumenges,
Quan no tenen res mes que fer,
Van a regar es claveller

Dihent-li: ¡Beu! ¡ja que no menjes!

The young girls, every Sunday,
When they have nothing more to do,
Go and water the carnation,
Telling it: Drink, since you do not eat!

The tune that accompanies the young girl's words has a Moorish rhythm, in a sad tone that haunts you and makes you dream. While the mother, who has understood what the girl means, is quick to answer her:

Atlotes, ¡filau! filau!
Que sa camya se riu;
Y sino l'apadassau,
¡No v's arribar a s'estiu!

Girls, spin! spin!
For your shift is breaking
              (literally, it is smiling)
And if you don't mend it
It won't last to the summer.

Mallorquin, especially from the mouths of women, has a particularly gentle and graceful charm to a ear of a foreigner. When a Mallorquin woman speaks these words of farewell, so softly melodious:

'Bona nit tenga! Es meco no basta per dir li: Adios!'

Good night! I have not the heart to say: Good bye!

It seems as if one could write down the soft notes as a phrase of music.

After these examples of the common Mallorquin language, I will allow myself to quote an example from the ancient scholarly language. This is the 'Mercader Mallorqui' (the Mallorquin merchant), a fourteenth century troubadour, who sings of the cruelties of his lady and then takes leave of her:

> Cercats d'uy may ja siats bella e pros
> 'quels vostres pres, e laus, e ris plesents,
> Car vengut es lo temps que m'aurets mens,
> No m'aucira vostre 'sguard amoros,
>
> > Ne la semblanca gaya
> > Car trobat n'ay
> > Altra qui m'play
> > Sol qui lui playa!
>
> Altra, sens vos, per que l'in volray be.
> E tindr' en car s'amor, que 'xi s'conve.

Search therefore, even though you are beautiful and proud,

Those merits, those praises, those charming smiles that were only for you,

For the time has come when you will seldom have me near you,

Your look of love can no longer kill me,

> Nor your false gaiety;
> For I have found
> Another who pleases me;
> If only I can please her!

Another, no longer you, for whom I would be grateful,

Whose love would be dear to me; that is what I must do.

The Mallorquins, like all Southern people, are natural musicians and poets, or as their ancestors called them, troubadours, 'trobadors'. which we would translate as improvisors. The island of Mallorca still has several who have a well deserved reputation, among others two who live in Soller. It is usually lovers, whether fortunate or unfortunate, who come to these 'trobadors'. Depending on the price and following the instructions they have been given, the troubadours stand under the girl's balcony late at night to sing improvised 'coplas' in a tone of praise or complaint and sometimes even of abuse, as they have been asked to do by the person who paid them. Foreigners can also treat themselves to this pleasure; on the island of Mallorca, this is not considered of any consequence. (M. Tastu's Notes.)

CHAPTER THREE

I cannot continue my narrative without concluding my examination of the religious records of Valldemossa for speaking of the fanatic piety of the villagers with whom we came in contact, I must mention the saint of whom they were so proud and whose simple house they showed us.

'Valldemossa is the home of Catalina Tomas, who was beatified in 1792 by Pope Pius VI. The life of this saintly girl has been written several times, and most recently by Cardinal Antonio Despuig. The story has some charmingly naive features. God, according to the legend, favoured his servant with judgment beyond her years. She was seen to rigorously observe the days of fasting long before the age when the Church demanded it. From a very early age she refrained from eating more than one meal a day. Her devotion to the Passion of the Redeemer and the suffering of the Holy Mother was so fervent that she continuously recited the rosary as she walked, using olive leaves or lentisk to count the decades. Her taste for seclusion and withdrawal for religious exercises and her aversion to dances and normal amusements, earned her the nickname of 'viejecita', the little old woman, but her loneliness and abstinence were rewarded by visits from angels and the entire company of heaven. Jesus Christ, His Mother and the Saints became her servants; Mary nursed her when she was sick; Saint Bruno raised her when she fell; Saint Antony accompanied her in the darkness of the night, carrying her pitcher and filling it at the well; Saint Catherine, her patron saint, arranged her hair and took care of everything for her, like an attentive and protective mother; Saint Cosmo and Saint Damian healed the wounds she received during her battles with the devil, for her victory did not come without a fight; and finally Saint Peter and Saint Paul stood by her side to assist her and defend her against temptation.

She embraced the rule of Saint Augustine at the monastery of Saint Magdalena in Palma and became an example to her sisters and, as the Church sings in its prayers, she was 'obedient, poor, chaste and humble.' Her biographers attribute to her the power of prophesy and the gift of miracles. They report that one day when public prayers were being said in Mallorca for the health of Pope Pius V, Catalina suddenly interrupted to say that it was no longer necessary because the Pontiff had departed from this world at that very hour, which was found to be true.

She died on 5th April 1574, saying these words from the psalm: 'Lord, into Thy hands, I commend my spirit.'

Her death was regarded as a public disaster; she was given the highest honours. A devout Mallorquin lady, Donna Juana de Pochs, replaced the wooden coffin in which the saintly girl had originally been laid, with a magnificent, alabaster one that she order-ed from Genoa. She also requested that masses be said for her on the day of her blessed translation and on the day of her patron saint, Saint Catherine. She asked for a lamp to burn perpetually on her tomb.

The body of this saintly girl is preserved today in the Convent of Saint Eulalia, where Cardinal Despuig has consecrated an altar and a religious service for her. [1]

I have happily related this little story in full, becau-se it does not enter at all into my ideas to deny the true sanctity and quality of passionate souls. Although the enthusiasm and the visions of the little mountain girl of Valldemossa will never have the same religious significance or the same value as the

[1] M. Tastu's notes.

inspirations and exstasies of the saints from the great era of Christianity, The 'Viejecita Tomasa' is no less than a sisterly cousin of the poetic shepherdess Saint Genevieve and the sublime shepherdess Saint Joan of Arc. The Roman Church has never refused to make a place of honour in the Kingdom of Heaven for the most humble children of the people; but the time has come when she condemns and rejects those apostles who want to improve the position of the people in the Kingdom of the Earth. The 'pagesa' (1), peasant girl, Catalina, was 'obedient, poor, chaste and humble'; The 'pages' of Valldemossa have learned so little from her example and understood so little of her life, that they once tried to stone my children because my son was sketching the ruins of the monastery, which they considered a desecration. They behaved like the Church who, with one hand, lit the pyres of the Inquisition, and with the other, lit incense on the tombs of the saints and the blessed.

The village of Valldemossa, which has been given

(1) 'Pages', 'pagesa', the name given to the men and women of the second class in Mallorca. The first class, 'es cavallers', are the knights or nobles; the second, 'es pagesos', the farmers; and the third, 'es menestrals', the artisans. All those who live and work on the land are called 'pages.'

(2) The Arabs called it Villa-Avente, a Roman name, which I believe was given to it by the Pisans of the Genoese.

the right to be called a town since Moorish times(2), is situated in the lap of the mountain, level with the Charterhouse, so that it resembles an annex. It is a cluster of sea swallows' nests; it is in an almost inaccessible site and the inhabitants are predominantly fishermen who leave in the morning and don't return until night. All day long, the village is filled with women, the most talkative in the world, and one sees them on the doorsteps busy mending their husband's nets or his hose, singing at the tops of their voices. They are as religious as the men, but their devotion is more tolerant because they are more sincere. In this, they are superior to the men, here like everywere else. Generally, the women practise their religion with enthusiasm, from habit and conviction, whereas with the men, it is more often a matter of ambition or advantage. France has provided quite strong proof that, during the reign of Louis XVIII and Charles X, both large and small positions in the government and in the army could be bought with a confession ticket or a mass.

The Mallorquin's attachment to the monks is founded on greed; and I can do no better to explain this than to quote M. Marliani, whose opinion is all the more valid because this historian of modern Spain generally showed himself to be against the action taken in 1835, that resulted in the sudden expulsion of the monks.

'Considerate landowners,' he says, 'and careless of their wealth, they created considerable interests between themselves and the peasants; the farmers that cultivated the monastery lands didn't have to struggle very hard, either with the amount or with the regularity of their rental payments. The monks, with no concern for posterity, didn't hoard their wealth and as soon as they possessed enough to pay for the material needs of each of them, proved to be very accomodating with the rest. Therefore the sudden plunder of the monks damaged the idle and egoistic calculations of the peasants: they soon realised that the Government and the new owners would be more careful than a community of parasites with no interest in family or in society. The beggars that swarmed at the doors of the refectory no longer cleaned up the unfinished remains of the meals.

The Carlist tendencies of the Mallorquin peasant can only be explained by material interests: for it would be impossible to find a province with fewer patriotic feelings towards Spain or with a population less excited by politics. Amidst their secret wishes for the restoration of the old regime, they were terrified by all new changes, whatever they were, and the alert that had put the island in a state of siege, at the time of our visit, startled the partisans of Don Carlos in Mallorca as much as defenders of Queen Isabella. Their alarm describes very well, I won't say the cowardice of the Mallorquins (I believe that they would be quite capable of making good soldiers), but their anxiety, caused by their concern for their property and their egoistic desire for peace.

An old priest dreamed one night that his house was invaded by brigands. He woke up in fright, under the effects of his nightmare, and woke his servant; who shared his terror and, without knowing what had caused it, woke the whole neighbourhood with her screams. Terror spread all over the village and from there all over the island. The news that a Carlist army had landed filled everyone's mind, and the Captain General received the testimony of the priest who, either ashamed to retract his statement or still deluded by the shock, assured him that he had seen the Carlists. All precautions were taken to confront the danger: Palma was declared in a state of siege, and all the military forces on the island were placed on alert.

Meanwhile nothing happened. No bush stirred, no foreign foot prints were seen, as on Robinson Crusoe's island, imprinted in the sand on the shore. The authorities punished the poor priest for making them look ridiculous, but instead of sending him abroad as a visionary, they sent him to prison as an agitator. But the precautionary measures were not revoked and when we left Mallorca at the time of the Maroto executions, the state of siege was still in force.

It was very strange the way the Mallorquins seemed to want to create a sense of mystery around some of the events that were disrupting the face of Spain at that time. No-one spoke of them, except within the family or in a hushed voice. In a country where there was really no wickedness or tyranny, it was extraordinary to see such widespread and suspicious mistrust. I have always regretted that I didn't bring some copies with me as example of Mallorquin polemic. But here, without exaggeration, is the form in which they would comment, after realising the facts, on their meaning and authenticity:

'However true these events might appear in the eyes of the people who are prepared to welcome them, we cannot recommend strongly enough that our readers await the results before judging them. The thoughts that come to mind in the presence of such events demand that a mature person waits to be certain, which we would not want to put in doubt, but which we would not take upon ourselves to hasten by making unwise assumptions. The destiny of Spain is covered in a veil which will soon be lifted, but it must not be lifted by an imprudent hand befire the time. We will refrain from giving their opinion on the actions of the various parties, until they have seen the situation more clearly,' etc.

Prudence and reserve are, according to the Mallorquins, the dominant traits of their character.

The peasants never met us in the countryside without exchanging a greeting with us; but if we said one word too many, without being known to them, they were certain not to reply, even when we spoke their dialect. It was enough that you appeared to be a foreigner for them to fear you and to go out of their way to avoid you.

However we would have lived on good terms with these worthy people if we had made an appearance in their church. We would still have been overcharged on every occasion, but we could have walked in their fields without the risk of being hit on the head by some stone from behind a bush. Unfortunately, this prudent action didn't enter our heads at the beginning and we remained almost until the end of our stay without realising how much our way of life scandalised them. They called us pagans, Mohammedans and Jews, which were the worst of all according to them. The mayor pointed us out to his people as a subject for his sermons. My daughter's shirt and trousers also offended them. They considered it very bad that a 'young person' of nine year's old ran around the mountains, 'disguised as a man'. It was not only the peasants who acted so prudishly.

On Sundays, the cow-horn that sounded in the village and along the lanes to call the latecomers to the service, pursued us in the Charterhouse in vain. We were deaf to it beacuse we didn't understand, and when we did understand, we were even more deaf to it. They had a way of avenging the glory of God however, which was not at all Christian. They were in league with each other and refused to sell us their fish, eggs and vegetables, except at exorbitant prices. They wouldn't let us question any bill, or any value. At the slightest objection, the peasant would ask with the air of a Spanish grandee: 'Don't you want it?' as he put his onions or his potatoes back into his bag. 'Then you won't have any,' and he would retire majestically. It would be impossible to get him to return and come to an agreement. He would make us starve to punish us for bargaining.

We did in fact have to starve. There was no rivalry or competition among the vendors. The one that came next would demand double, and the third demanded three times as much, so we were at their mercy and had to lead the lives of hermits, but at greater expense than living the life of a prince in Paris. We had the means of getting provisions from Palma through the French Consul's cook, who was our saviour and if I had been a Roman Emperor, I would have placed his cotton bonnet among the stars. But on rainy days, no messenger would risk travelling on the roads, at whatever price; and as it rained for two months, we often had bread as hard as ship's biscuits and dined like true Carthusians.

It would have been a small problem if we had all

been in good health. I am very sparing and even stoical by nature with regard to meals. The glorious appetites of my children took advantage of every opportunity and made a feast of every green lemon. My son, who had arrived weak and sickly, returned to life like a miracle and cured a serious rheumatic infection by running from morning till night, like an escaped hare, through the tall mountain vegetation, soaked to the waist. Providence allowed nature to perform these miracles for him. It was quite enough to have one invalid.

But the other one, far from prospering in the damp air and with all the hardships, worsened to an alarming extent. Although he had been condemned by the entire medical faculty of Palma, he didn't have a chronic infection, but the absence of a strengthening diet had thrown him, after a bad cold, into a weakened state from which he couldn't seem to recover. He resigned himself, as one can become resigned on one's own, but we couldn't resign ourselves to his state and I learned for the first time what great sorrows can be felt for such tiny difficulties, the fury of a peppery soup or a soup pilfered by the servants, the anxiety over the fresh bread that doesn't arrive or that is turned into a sponge by crossing a stream on the flanks of a mule. I certainly don't remember what I ate in Pisa or in Trieste, but I will live a hundred years before I forget the arrival of the basket of provisions at the Charterhouse. What I wouldn't have given to have had a rich broth and a glass of Bordeaux to offer our invalid every day! Mallorquin food and more than anything the way it was prepared, when we weren't attending to it or taking a hand in it, disgusted him. Should I tell you to what extent his disgust was well founded? One day, when we were served a thin chicken, we saw enormous '*Maître Flob*' jumping about on its smoking back, which Hoffman could have made into so many evil spirits, but which he certainly wouldn't have wanted to eat in a sauce. My children took it with such good, childish humour that they almost fell under the table.

The basis of Mallorquin cooking is invariably the pig, in every form and in all its aspects. That was the timely comment of the little Savoyard (slang for chimnet sweep, boot black) in praise of his cheap eating house, saying proudly that they ate five kinds of meat there, namely: pig meat, pork, lard, bacon and salted pork. In Mallorca, I am sure, they make more than two thousand different dishes with pork and at least two hundred types of sausage. Seasoned with so much garlic, pepper, pimento and corrosive spices of every sort, that one risks one's life with every bite. You see twenty dishes appearing on the table that resemble every kind of Christian food: don't trust them however; they are hellish stuff cooked by the devil himself. Finally, a pastry tart appears for dessert, that looks very good, with slices of fruit that look like candled oranges; it is a pork pie with garlic, with slices of 'tomatigas', or love apples, and peppers, the whole thing sprinkled with white salt that you took to be sugar, by its innocent appearance. There are lots of chickens, but they are no more than skin and bone. In Valldemossa, every grain we were sold to fatten them would no doubt have been taxed a 'real'. The fish they brought us from the sea was as flat and as dry as the chickens.

One day we bought a 'calmar', a squid of a large size in order to examine it. I have never seen a more horrible creature. Its body was as fat as a turkey, its eyes as large as oranges and its arms flabby and hideous, unwound, they were four or five feet long. The fishermen assured us that it was a delicacy. We were not at all tempted by its appearance and we presented it to Maria Antonia, who prepared it and tasted it with delight.

If our interest in the squid made these good people smile, we had our turn a few days later. Coming down from the mountain, we saw the farm workers leaving their work an approaching some people stopped in the road, who were carrying a pair of birds in a basket. They were wonderful, extraordinary, marvallous, incomprehensible. The whole population of the mountain were amazed by the appearance of these unknown fluttering birds. 'What do they eat?' they asked each other, watching them. And some of them replied: 'Maybe they don't eat.'

'Do they live on land or on the sea?' 'They probably live in the air all the time.' Finally, the two birds were nearly suffocated by the admiration of the public, until we verified they were neither condors, nor phoenixes, nor 'hippogriffes', (winged horses), but two beautiful farmyard geese that a wealthy lord was sending to one of his friends as a present.

In Mallorca, as in Venice, the liqueur wines are abundant and exquisite. We had a muscatel for every day use, as good and as inexpensive as the Cyprius wine that is drunk on the Adriatic coast. But the red wines, the preparation of which is truly an art, and unknown to the Mallorquins, are harsh, dark, burning, highly alcoholic and cost more than our simplest table wines in France. Alle these fiery and heady wines disagree with our invalid, and even with us, so much so that we almost always drank the water, which was excellent. I don't know if it was the purity of this spring water to which we could attribute the fact that we soon noticed that our teeth had acquired a whiteness which all the cosmetic art couldn't give to the most elegant Parisians. Perhaps our enforced sobriety was the cause.

With no butter and unable to stand the fat, the nauseating oil and the incendiary cooking methods of the Mallorquins, we lived on very lean mean, fish and vegetables, everything seasoned, in the form of a sauce, with the water of the stream with which we sometimes had the luxury of mixing the juice of a green orange, freshly picked from our garden. On the other hand, we had splendid desserts: sweet potatoes from Malaga and candied pumpkin from Valencia, and grapes worthy of the land of Canaan. These grapes, white and red, are oblong and with rather thick skins that help to conserve them all year round. They are exquisite and one can eat as many as one wishes without suffering from flatulance of the stomach, which ours give us. The grapes of Fontainebleau are watery and fresh; those of Mallorca are sweet and plump. One is for eating, the other is for drinking. These grapes, some of which weight twenty to twenty-five pounds, would win the admiration of a painter. They sustained us in times of food shortage. The peasants thought that they were selling them to us for a very high price, for they made us pay four times their value, but they didn't know that, compared to ours, it was still nothing and we both had the pleasure of laughing at each other. But, as far as the cactus figs were concerned, there was no question, they were the most detestable fruit that I know of.

If the conditions of this frugal lifestyle were difficult, and even disastrous to one of us, the others, I repeat, found it very acceptable in itself. We had succeeded, even in Mallorca, even in an abandoned Charter-house, even up against the most cunning peasants in the world, to create for ourselves a certain degree of well-being. We had window panes, doors and a stove, unique of its kind, that the best blacksmith in Palma had taken a month to forge and that cost us a hundred francs. It was quite simply an iron cylinder with a pipe that passed through the window. It required at least an hour to light it, and as soon as it became red and after leaving the doors open for a long time to let the smoke escape, it was necessary to reopen them almost immediately to let the heat out. Also, the so-called stove expert had lined the interior with, instead of cement, the material with which the Indians lined their houses and even their bodies for religious reasons, the cow being sacred to them, like one refers to a sacred animal. However purifying to the soul this saintly odour might be, I can tell you that in the fire place, it is hardly pleasing to the senses. For the month that the cement took to dry, we could have believed that we were in one of those circles in hell, where Dante claims to have seen the adulterers. I have really searched my memory for some mistake of that kind that would merit a similar punishment, what Power I have angered, what Pope or what king I have encouraged to err by my flattery; I haven't found an office boy or a porter of the Chamber on my conscience, not even a curtsy to policeman or a journalist!

Happily, the chemist at the Charterhouse sold us some exquisite Gum-Benzoin, the remainder of a supply of perfumes used to burn as incense in the monastery church, before the image of the Divinity, and this smell victoriously conquered the fumes from the eighth ditch of hell, in our cell.

We had splendid furniture; irreproachable trestle beds, sparsely stuffed mattresses, which were more expensive than in Paris, but new and clean, and those excellent, large bed covers in padded and stitched calico, that the Jews sold quite cheaply in Palma. A french lady, who lived on the island, was good enough to lend us several pounds of feathers, which she ordered for herself from Marseille, with which we had two pillows made for our invalid. It was certainly a great luxury in a country where geese are considered fastastic beings, and where the chickens are still itching even when they come off the skewer.

We had several tables, several straw chairs like the ones seen in our peasant's cottages, and a voluptuous white wood sofa with cushions covered in mattress ticking and stuffed with wool. The floor to the cell, that was very uneven and very dusty, was covered with those Valencian rush mats of long straw, that resembled grass yellowed by the sun, and with those beautiful, long haired sheep skins of a fine quality and whiteness, which they prepare so well in Mallorca.

Like the African and Oriental houses, there are no

cupboards in the old Mallorquin homes and particularly in the cells of the Charterhouse. Possessions are locked into huge white wood chests. Our yellow leather trunks could pass as very elegant furniture there. A large, multicoloured, tartan shawl, that we had used as a foot rug on the journey, bacame a sumptuous curtain in front of the alcove and my son decorated the stove with one of those charming pottery urns from Felanitx, which has a shape and decoration that is pure Arabic in style.

Felanitx is a village in Mallorca that ought to provide the whole of Europe with these lovely vases which are so light that they appear to be made of cork and are made with such fine clay that one could believe it to be a precious material. Exquisite little vases are also made there, which serve as water jugs and keep the water wonderfully cool. The clay is so porous that the water seeps through the sides of the vase and in less than half a day the vase is empty. I am the worst physicist in the world and perhaps the remark I have made is very foolish, although to me it seems wonderful and my pottery vase often seemed to be enchanted. We would leave it full of water on the stove, when the iron table was almost red, and sometimes when the water escaped through the pores of the vase, the vase was left dry on that burning plate and it never broke. Even when it only contained one drop of water, the water would be ice cold, even though the heat of the stove had blacked the wood we had put on the top of it.

That pretty vase, surrounded by a garland of ivy picked from the wall outside, was more satisfying to the eyes of an artist than all the gilt on our modern Sevres pocelain. The Pleyel piano, plucked from the hands of the customs officials after three weeks of negotiations and a contribution of four hundred francs, filled the high vaulted ceilings and resounded in the cell with a magnificent sound. The sacristan finally agreed to carry a beautiful, large, Gothic chair into our cell, sculpted in oak, which the rats and worms were gnawing away in the ancient Carthusian chapel. The box served us as a library at the same time as its delicate fret work and its tapering spires, projected onto the wall by the light of the lamp in the evening, reflected its rich, black lace work and its magnified turrets, and restored the ancient monastic character to our cell.

Señor Gomez, our ex-landlord from 'Son Vent', that wealthy individual who rented us his house in secret, because it wasn't considered respectable that a Mallorquin citizen appeared to be speculating on his property, made a scene and threatened legal action because we had broken a few earthenware plates in his house, that he made us pay for as if they had been Chinese porcelain. He also made us pay (always with threats) for the painting and repair of the whole of his house because of the contagious chest infection. Sometimes bad luck is good, for he forced us to buy the house linen that we had rented and as he was impatient to get rid of everything we had touched, he didn't forget to wrangle until we had paid for his old linen as if it was new. So thanks to him, we were not forced to sow flax so that one day we could have sheets and table clothes, like the Italian nobleman who granted shirts to his peasants. (pages??)

You must not accuse me of childishness because I decribe the problems for which surely I feel any more resentment that I feel regret for the loss to my purse. But nobody would disagree that the most interesting thing to observe in a foreign country is the people; and when I say that I did not have a single financial arrangement, however small, with the Mallorquins without discovering bad faith, indiscretion and an ugly greed on their part, and when I add that they flaunted their devotion in front of us, pretending to be indignant by our lack of faith, you will agree that the piety of simple souls, so vaunted by certain conservatives these days, is not always the most edifying and the most moral in the world, and that we must be allowed to hope for another way of understanding and honouring God. As for myself, I am so tired of hearing these common views: that it is criminal and dangerous to attack a false and corrupt faith because there is nothing to put in its place; that only people who are not infected with poisonous philosophical debate and revolutionary frenzy are moral, hospitable and sincere. That they still have the poetry and the grandeur of ancient virtues, etc. etc.!... I laughed in Mallorca a bit more than elsewhere, I can assure you, about these serious objections. When I saw my little children, brought up in that terrible abomination of desolation that is philosophy, cheerfully helping and assisting a suffering soul, all by themselves, among a hundred and sixty thousand Mallorquins who closed up and turned away, with the most hard hearted inhumantiy and with the most cowardly terror, against an invalid reputed to be contagious, I would say that those little scoundrels have more sense and charity that that entire population of saints and apostles.

Those pious servants of God didn't fail to tell me that I was committing a great crime by exposing my children to the infection, and that to punish me for my blindness, Heaven would give them the same disease. I told them that in our family, if one of us had the plague, the others would not throw away his bed; that it wasn't the custom in France, even less since the Revolution than before it, to abandon the sick; that Spanish prisoners, affected with the most terrible and dangeous diseases, had crossed our country during the Napoleonic wars and that our peasants, after sharing their food and their sheets with them, offered them their beds and after feeling obliged to care for them, that several had become victims of their own enthusiasm. The Mallorquin shook his head and smiled in pity, the idea of self sacrifice to an unknown stranger would no more enter into his head than honesty or even kindness towards a foreigner.

All the travellers who have visited the centre of the island were amazed however by the hospitality and selflessness of the Mallorquin farmer. They have written that if there were no inns in the country, it couldn't be easier and more agreeable to tour the countryside when a 'simple recommendation' was enough to be received, lodged and feted for nothing. That 'simple recommendation' is quite important, it seems to me. These travellers forget to say that all the classes in Mallorca, and in fact, all the inhabitants share a solidarity of interests that establishes good and easy relations between them, where religious charity and human sympathy do not count for nothing. A few words will explain this financial situation.

The nobles are rich in capital, poor in income and ruined by their debts. The Jews, who are numerous and rich in available money, have all the lands of the nobles in their pockets and one could say that the island belongs to them. The knights are no more than noble representatives, expected to do the honours for each other and for the occasional foreigner that lands on the island, in their estates and their palaces. To fulfil these elevated functions with dignity, they have to borrow every year from the Jew's exchange and every year the snowball gets bigger. I have alrea-

dy explained that the income from the land is paralysed by the lack of prospects and industry; meanwhile it is a point of honour among the poor nobles
to achieve their ruin slowly and pleasantly without
forfeiting their luxuries, it would be better to say, by
the detitute lavishness of their ancestors.

Therefore the farmer, who perhaps finds some
benefit in this division of his debts, pays his master
as little as possible and his banker as much as he can.
The lord is dependent and resigned, the Jewis relentless and patient. He makes concessions, he pretends
to be tolerant, he gives them time, but he pursues his
goal with diabolical genius; ever since he put his
claws into the landowner, piece by piece, everything
must come to him, and his interest will be necessary
to him until the debt reaches the value of the capital.
In twenty years there will be no landed nobility left
in Mallorca. The Jews could put themselves in power,
as they have done in France, and raise their heads
again after having been bowed and humiliated
hypocritically by the badly disguised scorn of the
nobles and the puerile and impotent fear of the people. In the meantime, they are the true landowners
and the peasants tremble before them. They turn
sadly to their old master and 'crying with tenderness'
they cheat him out of the last of his fortune. It is in their
interest to satisfy both powers and even to humour
them in everything, so that they won't be crushed between the two.

So if you are recommended to a peasant, either by a noble or by a wealthy man (and what other way could you be, when there is no middle class?), the peasant's door will immediately be opened to you. But try to ask for a glass of water without a recommendation and you will see!

And yet the Mallorquin peasant has gentleness, kindness, pleasant manners, a calm and patient nature. He dislikes evil, but he doesn't understand good. He goes to confession, he prays, he worries endlessly that he will be deserving of paradise, but he ignores the real obligations of humanity. He is no more detestable than an ox or a sheep, but he is no more of a man than these creatures asleep in their rough innocence. He recites his prayers, he is as superstitious as a savage but he would eat his fellow man without remorse if it was the custom of his country and if there was not enough pig meat to spare. He cheats, he overcharges, he lies, insults and robs, without the slightest embarrassment to his conscience. The foreigner is not really a man as far as he is concerned. He would never remove an olive from his neighbour but on the other side of the sea, human beings only exist on God's earth to provide a nice little profit for the Mallorquins.

We nicknamed Mallorca 'The island of Monkeys' because, seeing ourselves surrounded by these sneak-ing creatures, thieving yet innocent, we became accustomed to protecting ourselves from them with no more resentment or contempt than the Indian would feel towards the shy and roguish pongos and orang-utans.

All the same, one cannot get used to seeing, without feeling sad, animals dressed in human form and marked with a divine seal, vegetating like this in a world which is hardly that of present day humanity. One feels that this imperfect being is capable of understanding that his race could be improved, that his prospects are the same as those of more advanced races and that it is only a question of time, a long time from our point of view, but hardly noticeable in the space of eternity. But the more one has a feeling for this perfectibility, the more one suffers at the sight of these people, shackled in the chains of the past. This interruption doesn't worry Providence in the least, even though it spoilt and upset our existence at the time. We feel in our heart, in our mind and on our guts that the lives of others are connected with our own, that we cannot survive without loving and being loved, understanding and being understood, helping and being helped. The idea of an intellectual and moral superiority over other men only pleases the hearts of the proud. I imagine that all generous hearts would prefer rather than lowering themselves to the same level, to raise in a blink of an eye all those who are beneath them. So that they can live at last a true life of sympathy, intercourse, equality and communication, which is the religious ideal of the human conscience.

I am certain that this need is at the bottom of every heart and that those of us who fight it and try to suffocate it with fallacies, experience a strange and bitter pain, for which they cannot find a name. The men underneath become worn and burn themselves out when they cannot climb higher, those on top feel indignant and hurt when they stretch out their hand in vain, and those who don't want to help anyone are devoured with boredom and the dread of loneliness until they fall back into a brutality that causes them to fall lower than the lowest.

CHAPTER FOUR

So we were alone in Mallorca, as isolated as if we had been in a desert, and when we had won our daily rations by waging war against the 'monkeys', we sat down together around the stove to laugh about it. But as the winter advanced, the sadness in my heart paralysed every effort to be cheerful and calm. The health of our invalid continued to get worse; the wind cried down the ravine, the rain battered against our windows, the voice of the thunder penetrated our thick walls and threw a mournful note amidst the laughter and games of the children. The eagles and vultures, encouraged by the mist, came and devoured our poor sparrows right over the pomegranate tree that filled my window. The angry sea kept the boats from leaving the ports; we felt like prisoners, far from intelligent help and useful sympathy. Death seemed to be hovering over our heads, waiting to take one of us, and we were alone in fighting to save him. There was not a single human creature within reach who would not have preferred, on the contrary, to push him closer to the tomb, to rid themselves more quickly of the imaginary danger of his presence. This hostile feeling was dreadfully sad. We felt quite strong enough to replace with care and self sacrifice, the help and sympathy that was denied us; I also believe that in this kind of situation, the heart expands and affection increases, strengthened by all the force it derives from the feeling of human solidarity. But we suffered in our hearts to find ourselves thrown into the midst of people who didn't understand that feeling, and far from complaining about them, we couldn't help feeling the most painful pity towards them.

I also experienced some violent confusion. I have no scientific knowledge of any sort, and I would have had to be a doctor, and a great doctor, to have known how to treat that illness, the responsibility of which weighed on my heart.

The doctor who saw us, and I do not question his zeal or his talent, was mistaken, like all doctors, even the most famous, can be mistaken and as he said himself, all honest experts are often mistaken. Bronchitis had been followed by a nervous condition that has produced many of the symptoms of laryngeal consumption.

The doctor who had seen these symptoms at certain times and had not seen any contrary symptoms, which had been obvious to me at other times, prescribed a treatment suitable for comsumptives, namely bleeding, a low diet and a milk diet. All these things were totally inadvisable and bleeding would have been fatal. The invalid knew this instinctively, and without knowing anything about medicine, but having nursed many invalids, I had the same feeling. I trembled however at the thought of relying on an instinct that could be mistaken and of resisting the assurances of a man of experience; and when I saw the illness getting worse, I was really relieved from my anxiety, as anyone could understand. 'A bleeding would save him,' I was told, 'and if you refuse to allow it, he is going to die.' Yet there was a voice that told me, even in my sleep: 'Bleeding will kill him, and if you save him from it, he won't die.' I was certain that the voice was the voice of Providence, because today, our friend, the terror of the Mallorquins, is recognised as being no more consumptive than I am, I thank Heaven for not letting me doubt the courage that saved us.

As far as the low diet was concerned, it was very unfavourable. When we saw the bad effect it was having on him, we followed it as little as possible, but unfortunately there was not much to choose between the hot local spices and the most frugal meals. Milk products, whose harmful effects we recognised later, were luckily very rare in Mallorca, because none are produced there. At that time we still thought that milk would work wonders and we tormented ourselves to get hold of it. There are no cows in those mountains and the goat milk they sold us was always drunk on the way by the children who brought it, which didn't prevent the jug from arriving even fuller than when it started. It was a miracle that was performed every morning by the pious messenger while he carefully said his prayers in the Charterhouse courtyard, right beside the well. To put an end to these wonders, we bought ourselves a goat. It was the most gentle and most lovable person in the world, a beautiful, little African goat, with short hair the colour of chamois, a head without horns, a very curved nose and drooping ears. Those animals were very different from ours. They have coats like a roe deer and the profile of a sheep, but they don't have the mischievous and obstinate nature of our playful female kids. On the contrary, they seem very melancholy. These goats also differ from ours in that they have very small udders and give very little milk. When they are fully grown, their milk has a sharp and bitter flavour, which the Mallorquins value highly but which seemed repulsive to us.

Our friend at the Charterhouse was having her first maternity; she wasn't two years old and her milk was very delicate, but she was very sparing with it, especially when she was separated from the herd to which she belonged, not to gamble (she was too serious, too Mallorquin for that) but to dream on top of the mountains, and she fell into a bad mood that was not unlike our own. There was in fact very good grass in the yard, and aromatic plants which had once been cultivated by the monks were still growing in the beds of our garden, but nothing consol-ed her in captivity. She wandered lost and desolate through the cloisters, emitting mournful bleats that would have cracked a stone. We gave her a very fat sheep for company, whose thick, white wool was six inches long, one of those sheep that we only see at home in front of toy-shops or on our grandmother's fan. Such excellent company made her a little calmer and she gave us quite creamy milk. But the two of them, however well fed, produced such a small quantity that we were suspicious of the frequent visits that Maria Antonia, the 'niña' and Catalina made to our livestock. We put them under lock and key in a little courtyard under the bell tower and we took care to milk them ourselves. This milk, which was very light, mixed with the milk of almonds which the children and I took turns to pick, made quite a healthy and pleasant drink. We didn't have anything else. All the medicines in Palma were unbearably unhygienic. The badly refined sugar which they bring from Spain, is black, oily and blessed with a purgative effect on anyone who isn't used to it.

One day, we thought we were saved because we noticed some violets in a garden belonging to a rich farmer. He allowed us to pick some in order to make an infusion, and as soon as we had made our little parcel, he asked us to pay one 'sou' per violet, A Mallorquin 'sou' which is worth three French 'sou'!

As well as these domestic worries we had to sweep our rooms and make our beds ourselves when we wanted to sleep at night, because the Mallorquin servant couldn't touch them without immediately transmitting to us, in intolerable profusion, the same objects that my children had found so amusing to see on the back of the roast chicken. It left us no more than a few hours to work and to go for a walk, but those hours were well spent. The children were attentive during the lesson and we had only to put our noses out of our den, to enter the most varied and delightful landscape. At every step, in the midst of that huge framework of mountains, an unexpected scene presented itself, a little chapel on a steep rock, a thicket of rhododendrons thrown precipitously on a hazardous slope, a hermitage over a spring, filled with tall reeds, a stand of trees on an enormous fragment of rock, covered with moss and embroidered with ivy. When the sun deigned to show itself for a moment all the plants and rocks and fields, washed by the rain, sparkled with shimmering colours and with unbelievably clear reflections.

We went on two particularly memorable walks. I don't have pleasant memories of the first, even though the views were magnificient. For our invalid, who was feeling well at that time (it was at the beginning of our stay in Mallorca) wanted to accompany us and as a result became exhausted which caused the onset of his illness.

Our destination was a hermitage situated on the sea coast, three miles from the Charterhouse. We followed the right branch of the mountain chain and climbed from hill to hill on a stony path that cut our feet, to the north coast of the island. At each turn of the path we had a magnificient view of the sea, seen from a considerable distance, over the most beautiful vegetation. It was the first time I had seen those fertile shores, covered with trees and greenery right up to the first wave, without pale cliffs or desolate beaches or a muddy strand. In all the coasts of France that I have seen, even on the heights of Port Vendres where the sea at last appeared to me in all its beauty, it has always seemed dirty and unpleasant to approach. The Lido in Venice, which is so highly praised, has terribly empty sands, populated with enormous lizards that come out in their throusands from under your feet and seem to be following you, with their number always increasing, like a bad dream. In Royant, in Marseilles, almost everywhere, I believe, along our coasts a belt of slimy seaweed and barren sands mar the approaches to the sea. In Mallorca, I saw the sea at last as I had dreamed of it, as clear and blue as the sky, gently undulating like a sapphire plain, evenly furrowed in ridges and hardly moving, seen from a certain height, and framed by dark green forests. Every step we took along the winding mountain presented us with a new perspective, each one more perfect than the last. Nevertheless, as we had to descend again to reach the hermitage, the shoreline in that area, although very beautiful, did not have the kind of grandeur that I found in another part of the coast a few months later.

The four or five hermits who had settled there had not created anything poetic. Their dwelling was miserable and rough, as their profession demands, and from their terraced garden, where we found them busy digging, the great loneliness of the sea stretched beneath their eyes. But they appeared to us personally the most stupid in the world. They didn't wear any religious dress. The superior left his spade and came towards us in a dress of beige material; his short hair and his dirty beard didn't look at all picturesque. He talked to us about the severity of the life he led and most of all about the unbearable cold that existed on that coast, but when we asked him if it ever froze there, we couldn't make him understand what frost was. He didn't know the word in any language and he had never heard of a country that was colder than the island of Mallorca. Yet he had an idea of France after seeing the fleet pass by in 1830 on their way to conquer Algiers. It had been the most beautiful, the most amazing, one would say the only spectacle of his life, he asked us if the French had

succeeded in taking Algiers and when we told him that they had just taken Constantine, he opened his eyes wide and cried that the French were a great nation.

He made us climb up to a small, very dirty cell where we saw the oldest of the hermits. We took him to be a hundred and were surprised to learn that he was only eighty. The man was in a perfect state of idiocy, although he continued to work, mechanically making wooden spoons with dirty, trembling hands. he took no notice of us at all, even though he was not deaf and when the prior called his name he lifted his enormous head, which one could have mistaken for wax, and showed us a face that was hideously degraded. There was a whole life of intellectual abasement in those distorted features,. for although I quickly turned my eyes away, it was the most horrifying and painful sight in the world. We gave them alms for they belong to a mendicant order and they are still highly revered by the peasants who do not leave them in need of anything.

Returning to the Charterhouse, we were confronted with a strong wind which blew us over several times and which made it so tiring to walk that our invalid was worn out by it.

The second walk took place before we left Mallorca and it made an impression on me that I will never for-

243

get in my life. Never has the sight of nature had such a positive effect on me and I don't think that I have been so impressed more than three or four times in my life.

The rain had stopped at last and spring had arrived all at once. We were in the month of February, all the almond trees were in blossom and the fields were filled with sweet scented jonquils. That was the only difference, apart from the colour of the sky and the brightnesss in the tones of the countryside, that the eye could find between the two seasons; for the trees in that region are almost always green. Those that come up early don't have to survive the frosts, the grass retains all its freshness, and the flowers only need one sunny morning to lift their noses into the air. While our garden was under half a foot of snow, the wind rocked the pretty little climbing roses on our trellised arbour and even though they were a bit pale, they didn't seem any less good humoured.

As I could see the sea, to the north, from the door of the monastery, one day when our invalid was feeling well enough to be left alone for two or three hours, the children and I set off at last to see the shore of that coast. Until then I had not had the least curiosity about it, although my children, who ran about like deer, assured me that it was the most beautiful place in the world. Either because the visit to the hermitage, the first cause of our misery, had left me feeling rather a deep resentment or because I didn't expect to see at sea level as beautiful a view of the sea as I had seen from up on the mountain, I had not yet felt any temptation to leave the small, enclosed valley of Valldemossa.

I explained earlier that, at the point where the Charterhouse stood, the mountain chain opened up and a gently rising plain rose between the two branches and widened towards the sea. Yet, looking at the sea every day rising to the horizon well above that plain, my eyes and my reason were making a curious mistake; instead of seeing that the plain rose and then stopped suddenly at the short distance from me, I imagined that it dropped gently to the sea and that the coast was more that five or six leagues away. How could I have known, in fact, that the sea that appeared to be level with the Charterhouse, was more than two or three thousand feet below? I was amazed sometimes that the sound could be so loud if it was as far away as I thought. I couldn't understand this phenomenon and I don't know how I can allow myself sometimes to mock the Parisian bourgoisie, when I am even more simpleminded in my ideas. I couldn't see that the horizon of the sea in front of my eyes was fifteen to twenty leagues from the coast, while the sea pounded the foot of the island half an hour's walk from the Charterhouse. So when my children asked me to come and see the sea, implying that it was two steps away. I never found the time, believing that it was a question of two child's steps, that is, in reality two steps of a giant; for we know that children walk with their heads, without remembering that they have feet, and that the seven league boots of Petit Poucet is a myth that signifies that children can travel around the world without realising it.

In the end, I was left trailing behind them, certain that we would never reach that fantastic shore that seemed so far away to me. My son considered that he knew the way, but as everything is a path when one has seven league boots and as, for a long time now, I no longer walk anywhere except in slippers I complained to him that I could no longer jump over ditches, hedges and streams, like he and his sister. For a quarter of an hour I had noticed that we were not descending towards the sea, for the course of the mountain streams came rapidly to meet us, and the more we advanced, the more the sea appeared to be receding and sinking towards the horizon. At last I thought we had turned our backs on it and I asked the first peasant I met if, by chance, it would be at all possible for us to find the sea.

Under a clump of willows in a muddy ditch, three shepherdesses, perhaps three fairies in disguise, were stirring the mud with shovels to find I don't know what talisman or salad. The first one had no more than one tooth, she was probably the Tooth Fairy, the same one that stirs her spells in a pot with this one, horrible tooth. The second old woman, by all appearances, was 'Carabosse', the most deadly enemy of orthopaedic surgery. They both made dreadful grimaces at us. The first one brought her terrible tooth closer to my daughter whose freshness wetted her appetite. The second one jerked her head and brandished her stick to break my son's back, because his straight, young body disgusted her. But the third, who was young and pretty, jumped lightly over the edge of the ditch and throwing her cape over her shoulders, motioned to us with her hand and began to walk away in front of us. She was obviously a good little fairy, but in her disguise as a mountaineer, she asked us to call her 'Perica de Pier Bruno'.

Perica is the kindest Mallorquin creature that I have seen. She and my goat are the only living souls in Valldemossa for whom I have kept a place in my heart. The little girl was so muddy that the little goat would have blushed, but when she had walked a short way over the damp grass, her bare feet became, not quite white, but as dainty as an Andalusian girls' and her pretty smile, her inquisitive and confident chatter and her unselfish kindness made us feel that we had discovered a fine pearl. She was sixteen years old and had the most delicate features with a smooth, rounded face like a peach. She had the balanced lines and beautiful proportions of a Greek statue. Her waist was as slim as a reed and her bare arms were a tanned colour. From under her 'rebozillo' of rough linen, her hair floated and tangled like the tail of a young filly. She led us to the edge of her land, then made us cross a sown field surrounded by trees and great blocks of rock; and I could no longer see the sea at all, which made me think that we were approaching the mountain and that the naughty Perica was making fun of us.

But suddenly she opened a small gate that closed off the field and we saw a path encircling a large sugarloaf rock. We followed the path and as if by magic, we found ourselves above the sea, above the vastness with another cliff a league away beneath our feet. The first reaction to this unexpected sight was a sense of vertigo and I started to sit down. Little by little I felt reassured and had the courage to descend the path, which had not been made for human feet but for goats. What I saw was so beautiful that for a moment I had, not seven league boots, but swallow's wings in my head; and I started off around the great limestone peaks, like giants a hundred feet high, along the face of the cliff, always looking for the bottom of the cove that plunged on my right out of the earth and where the fishing boats seemed as big as flies.

All at once, I could see nothing more in front of me and above me but the blue sea. The path had disap-

peared I don't know where; Perica called from above
my head and my children, who were following me
on all fours, decided to call even louder. I turned
round and saw my daughter in tears. I retraced my
steps to ask her what was wrong and, after a
moment's thought, I realised that the children's terror
and despair was not without reason. One more step
and I would have descended much faster than necessary, unless I had managed to walk upside down,
like a fly on the ceiling; for the rocks where I had
ventured overhung a little gulf and the base of the
island was deeply eroded beneath it. When I saw the
danger in which I would had led my children, I was
terribly frightened and I hurried to climb back to
them; but when I had put them safely behind one of
those sugarloaf mountains, I had another fit of desire
to see the bottom of the cove and underneath the cliff.

I have never seen anything like the scene that I
found there, and my imagination took off at a full
gallop. I went down another path, crouching in the
brambles and holding onto the stone peaks, where
each one marked a new path falling away. At last, I
began to catch a glimpse of the huge mouth of the
hollow, where the waves crashed with a strange
music. I don't know what magical notes I thought I
could hear, nor what unknown world I flattered myself that I had discovered, when my son, frightened
and a little angry, came and roughly pulled me back.
I was compelled to fall in the most unpoetic way in

the world, not forward, which would have been the end of the adventure and of my own, but sitting down like a sensible person. The child gave me such a lovely scolding that I abandoned the idea, but not without a feeling of regret that still haunts me, for every year my slippers become heavier and I don't think that the wings I had that day will ever grow again to carry me over similar shores.

It is true however, and I know this as well as anyone, that what one sees is seldom equal to what one dreams. But this is only true of the art and work of man. As far as I'm concerned, either my imagination is as lazy as usual or God is more talented than I am (which would not be impossible), but I have almost always found nature infinitely more beautiful than I expected, and I don't remember ever having found it disagreeable unless it was at a time when I was feeling that way myself.

So I will never forgive myself for not being able to climb around that rock. Perhaps I would have seen Amphitrite in person, under an arch of mother-of-pearl, with her forehead crowned with murmuring seaweed. Instead of that, I only saw the limestone peaks rising from gorge to gorge like stalactites, in cave after cave, and all taking on strange shapes and fantastic positions. Strong, healthy trees, but all crooked and partly uprooted by the winds, hung over the abyss, at the bottom of which another mountain rose in a peak up to the sky, a crystal mountain of diamonds and sapphires. The sea, seen from a great height, gives the impression, as everyone nows, of a vertical wall. Explain it, if you will.

My children decided that they wanted to take some plants. The most beautiful lilies in the world grew among these rocks. The three of us finally pulled up a bulb of glittering Amaryllis, that we couldn't carry as far as the Charterhouse, it was so heavy. My son cut it into pieces to show a fragment, as big as his head, of that marvellous plant to our invalid. Perica, laden with a large bundle of sticks that she had collected on the way, with which she kept knocking us on the nose by her hurried and clumsy movements, led us to the entrance of the village. I persuaded her to come as far as the Charterhouse to give her a little present, which I had a lot of trouble in making her accept. Poor little Perica, you don't know and you will never know what good you did to me by showing me one gentle, human creature among the monkeys, charming and helpful without a second thought. That evening, we all rejoiced that we were not leaving Valldemossa without having met one sympathetic person.

CHAPTER FIVE

Between the two walks, the first and the last we took in Mallorca, we made several others that I will not describe for fear of boring my reader with my monotonous enthusiasm for that countryside which is beautiful everywhere and sown all over with picturesque houses that compete with each other, cottages, palaces, churches, monasteries. If one of our great landscape painters ever decides to visit Mallorca, I recommend to him the country house of La Granja de Fortuny, with the valley of lemon trees that opens in front of the marble colonnade and the entire road that leads to it. But without going that far, he would not have to take ten steps into that enchanted island without stopping at each turn of the road, either before an Arabic cistern shaded with palm trees, or before a stone cross, the delicate work of the fifteenth century, or on the edge of a grove of olive trees.

Nothing equals the strength and the strangeness of

253

these ancient guardians of Mallorca. The Mallorquins say that the most recent were planted at the time of the Roman occupation of their island. I cannot contest that, not knowing any way of proving the contrary, even if I wanted to, and I assure you that I have not the slightest desire. To see the formidable appearance, immeasureable size and the enraged positions of these mysterious trees, my imagination would willingly have accepted them as contemporaries of Hannibal. When one walks in the evening under their shade, one really has to remind oneself that they are trees; for if one believed one's eyes and imagination, one would be terrorised by these fantastic monsters, some of which lean over you like huge dragons with gaping jaws and outstretched wings; others wind around themselves like swollen boa constrictors; while others furiously embrace each other like battling giants. Here is a galloping centaur carrying on its back I don't know what hideous ape; there a nameless reptile who is eating a gasping doe; further away, a satyr who is dancing with a goat, not nearly as ugly as himself; and often there is a solitary tree, split, knotted, twisted, humpbacked, which you take to be a group of ten distinct trees and which represents all these different monsters joined to one single head, as horrible as those Indian fetishes, and crowned with one single, green branch like a crest. Those curious enough to take a look at M. Laurens' plates need not fear that he has exaggerated the shapes of the olive trees that he has drawn. He could have chosen far more extraordinary examples, and I hope that the 'Magasin pittoresque', that amusing and tireless popularizer of the marvals of art and nature, will bring us, one morning soon, a few, first class specimens.

But to recreate the grandeur of these sacred trees, where one is always expecting to hear prophetic voices and the shining sky where their stark outlines are so vigorously drawn, requires nothing less than the bold, majestic brush of Rousseau[1]. The clear waters where daffodils and myrtles are reflected, call for Dupré. The more ordered places and where nature, although free, seems to have taken on, by an excess of coquetry, a proud and classic appearance, would tempt the severe Corot. But to recreate the adorable tangle, where a whole world of grasses, wild flowers, old logs and weeping garlands hang over a secret spring, where a stork comes to bathe his long legs, I would have liked to have had, like a magic wand at my disposal, Huet's engraving tool in my pocket.

How many times, seeing an old Mallorquin aristocrat alone in his palace, faded and dilapidated, have I dreamed of Decamps, the great master of serious caricature ennobled into a historic art, the man of genius

(1) *Rousseau, one of the greatest landscape painters of our time, is unknown to the public, thanks to the obstinate judges of painting, who for several years have denied him the right to exhibit his masterpieces.*

who knows how to create energy and gaiety, poetry and life itself, even in the walls? The beautiful, sun-tanned children who played in our cloister, wearing monk's costume, would have greatly amused him. He could have had as many monkeys as he liked there, and angels among the monkeys, pigs with human faces, then a cherubim mixed up with the pigs and just as dirty; Perica, as beautiful as Galatée, as muddy as a spaniel, and laughing in the sun like all that is beautiful on earth.

But it is you, Eugene, my old friend, my dear artist, whom I would like to have led into the mountains at night when the moon lit the dark flood. It was a beautiful countryside, where I was nearly drowned with my poor child of fourteen, but where he didn't lack courage, nor I the ability to see how nature, that evening, became supremely romantic, supremely crazy and supremely sublime.

We had left Valldemossa, the child and I, in the middle of the winter rains, to go and discuss the Pleyel piano with the ferocious customs officials in Palma. The morning had been quite clear and the roads were passable, but while we were running around the town, the adverse conditions became steadily worse. Here, we complain about the rain and we don't know what it is; our longest rains rarely last two hours; one cloud follows another and inbetween the two, there is always a moment of respite. In Mallorca, a permanent cloud covers the island and settles there until it is exhausted, which lasts forty, fifty hours, or four or five days, without any interruption or even any lessening of intensity.

We returned about sunset in the 'birlocho', expecting to reach the Charterhouse in three hours. We took seven, and we almost had to sleep with the frogs at the bottom of some improvised lake. The driver of the birlocho was in a murderous mood; he found a thousand excuses to avoid starting off on the journey; his horse was unshod, his mule was lame, the axle was broken, I don't know what else! We had begun to know the Mallorquin well enough not to feel defeated, and we persuaded him to climb onto his carriage, where he remained in the most unhappy frame of mind in the world for the first few hours. He didn't sing, he refused our cigars, he didn't even swear at his mule, which was a very bad sign; he was worried to death. Hoping to frighten us, he began by taking the worst of the seven routes known to him. The road dropped lower and lower and we soon encountered the stream and we went into it but we didn't come out of it. The good stream, ill at ease in its bed, had made a deviation across the road; and there was nothing more of the road but a river, where the water rushed towards us with a loud roar and at a great pace.

When the malicious driver, who had counted on

our faintheartedness, saw that we had made up our minds, he lost his temper and began to fume and swear, enough to bring down the vault of the heavens. The stone channels that carried the spring water to the town were so swollen that they had burst, like the frog in the fable. Then, not knowing where to go, they had overflowed into pools, then into ponds, then into lakes, then into the arms of the sea all over the countryside. Soon the driver no longer knew which saint to pray to, nor which devil to damn. His legs were soaked, which he well deserved and for which we felt in no position to pity him. The carriage closed very well and we were still dry; but minute by minute, according to my son, 'the tide was rising', we travelled at random, getting dreadfully jolted and falling into holes, the last of which always seemed certain to put us in the grave. We finally leaned over so far that the mule halted, as if to collect itself before giving up the ghost; the driver got up and tried to climb onto the edge of the road, which was at the height of his head; but he stopped when he recognised, in the glimmer of the twilight, that the edge was none other than the canal of Valldemossa, turned into a river, which from time to time, poured in a waterfall over the road, which had also flooded at a lower level.

Then there was a tragi-comic moment. I was a little frightened on my account and very afraid for my child. I looked at him; he was laughing at the sight of the driver who, standing up, his legs astride the shafts, was measuring the gap, with no longer the slightest desire to amuse himself at our expense. When I saw my son so relaxed and so cheerful, I revived my confidence in God. I realised that he had an instinct for survival and I trusted in that intuition that children don't know how to explain, but that spreads like a cloud or a ray of sunlight on their foreheads.

The driver, seeing that he didn't have any way of abandoning us to our miserable fate, resigned himself to sharing it and all at once became heroic: 'Don't be afraid, my children!' he said to us in a fatherly voice. Then he gave a loud cry and whipped his mule, who stumbled, fell, got up, stumbled again and got up at last half drowned. The carriage sank to one side: 'Here we are!' It fell over on the other side: 'Here we are again!' It made sinister creaks, fabulous bounds and emerged at last, triumphant from the ordeal, like a ship that has touched the rocks without breaking.

We appeared to be saved, we were dry, but it was necessary to begin that attempt at a nautical journey by carriage a dozen times before we climbed the mountain. At last, we reached the ramp, but there the mule, exhausted for one thing, and also frightened by the noise of the stream and the wind in the mountains, began to reverse towards the edge of the precipice. We got down, and each of us pushed a wheel, while the driver pulled Mister Aliboron by his long ears. We had to get down, I don't know how many times, and at the end of two hours of climbing, during which we didn't make half a league, the mule hung back on the bridge, trembling all over, and we made the decision to leave the man, the vehicle and the animal there and to reach the Charterhouse on foot.

That was no small achievement. The steep path was a violent torrent and it needed strong legs to fight against it. Other smaller streams, falling from the top of the rocks with a loud noise, appeared suddenly to our right and we often had to hurry to pass in front of them or to cross them at great risk, fearing that at any moment they would become impassable. The rain fell in waves; enormous clouds, blacker than ink, veiled the face of the moon at every moment, and then, enveloped in grey, impenetrable shadows, bowed down by the strong wind, feeling the tops of the trees bending down over our heads, hearing the creaking of the fir trees and the stones rolling down around us, we were forced to stop and listen, as the cunning poet has said, to know whether Jupiter had blown out the candle.

It was in those moments of darkness and light that you would have seen, Eugene, the sky and the earth grow paler and brighter in turns, with the most sinister and strange reflections and shadows. When the moon shone again and seemed to want to reign in a corner of the blue that was quickly swept before her by the wind, dark clouds came like ghosts determin-ed to wrap her in the folds of their shrouds. They hurried across her and sometimes tore apart to reveal her to us even more beautiful and more help-ful. The mountain running with waterfalls and the trees uprooted by the storm gave us an idea of the chaos. We thought of that beautiful sabbat that you saw in some dream and that you sketched with, I don't know what paintbrush, dipped in the red and blue waves of Phlegeton and Erebe. Just as we were contemplating this hellish picture that was in reality right in front of us, the moon, devoured by the monsters in the air, disappeared and left us in a blue black limbo, where we seemed to be floating like clouds, for we could not even see the ground where we dared to put our feet.

At last we reached the paved road of the last mountain and we were out of danger once we left the water course. Fatigue had exhausted us and we were barefoot, or very nearly. We had taken three hours to cover that last league.

But the good weather returned and the Mallorquin steamer could resume its daily runs to Barcelona. Our invalid didn't seem to be in a state to survive the crossing, but he seemed equally unable to support another week in Mallorca. The situation was dreadful; there were days when I lost hope and courage. To console us, Maria Antonia and her friends from the village, repeated in unison around us the most helpful advise about his future. 'That consumptive,' they would say, 'will go to hell, firstly because he is consumptive, then because he hasn't confessed. If that is so, when he is dead, we won't bury him in consecrated ground, and as no-one would want to give him a burial, his friends will have to arrange whatever they can. It remains to be seen how they will get out of that; for my part, I won't get involved.' 'Nor me.' 'Nor me. And amen!'

At last we left, and I have told you what society and what hospitality we found on the Mallorquin ship.

When we arrived in Barcelona, we were so impatient to be finished for all eternity with that inhuman race that I didn't have a patience to await the end of the disembarkation. I wrote a note to the commander of the station, M. Belvès, and it was sent to him by boat. A few minutes later, he came to fetch us in his barge and we went on board the 'Méléagre'.

As we set foot on that fine warship, kept as clean and as elegant as a sitting room, finding ourselves surrounded by intelligent and cheerful faces, receiving the generous and impressive attentions of the commander, the doctor, the officers and all the crew, on shaking hands with the excellent and intelligent French consul, M. Gautier d'Arc, we leapt with joy onto the bridge, crying from the bottom of our hearts: 'Vive la France!' It seemed as if we had made a tour of the world and left the savages of Polynesia for the civilised world.

And the moral of this story, childish perhaps but sincere, is that man is not made to live with the trees, with the stones and the clear sky, and the blue sea, with the flowers and the mountains, but with men, his fellow men.

In the stormy days of youth, one imagines that solitude is the great refuge against attack, the great remedy for the wounds of combat; it is a serious mistake, and experience of life teaches us that, where one cannot live in peace with one's fellow men, there is no admiration of poetry nor delight in art capable of filling the abyss that opens at the depth of the soul.

I have always dreamed of living in a desert, and all honest dreamers will confess that they have had the same fantasy. But believe me, my brothers, we have a heart too loving to pass each other by; and the thing we are left to do, is to support each other mutually; for we are like the children of the same breast, who tease and quarrel, and even fight and at the same time, cannot leave each other.

THE END

LIST OF ILLUSTRATIONS